Travellers' guide to Portugal

SUSAN LOWNDES

GEOGRAPHIA

Other titles in this series are:

Travellers' Guide to Egypt
Travellers' Guide to Greece
Travellers' Guide to Ireland
Travellers' Guide to Israel
Travellers' Guide to Malta, Gozo and Comino
Travellers' Guide to Southern Africa
Travellers' Guide to Southern France

Thornton Cox Travellers' Guides
Portugal
© Geographia Limited 1982
First published 1982

Text by Susan Lowndes
Drawings by Guy Magnus
Maps by Tom Stalker-Miller, M.S.I.A.
Cover photo: Pena Palace, Sintra

Geographia Limited
17–21 Conway St
London W1P 6JD

Great care has been taken throughout this
book to be accurate, but the publishers cannot
accept responsibility for any errors which appear

Set in Univers by Rowland Phototypesetting Ltd,
Bury St Edmunds, Suffolk

Colour separations by Dot Gradations Ltd, Chelmsford, Essex
Printed in Great Britain by The Guernsey Press Co Ltd
Guernsey, Channel Islands

ISBN 0 09 207960

Contents

Author's Acknowledgements

I am grateful to Senhora D. Maria Luisa Matos Ferreira who came with me to explore the Algarve again, and to my daughter Ana Marques Vicente who made helpful suggestions.

I would also like to acknowledge my indebtedness in the writing of this book, not only to Mrs W. D. Thorburn, who has typed and retyped with the greatest patience and added much to my knowledge of Tras-os-Montes, where she was brought up, but to the staffs of the many local tourist offices who eagerly answered my questions and the custodians of museums, who communicated to me their pride and pleasure in the objects under their care, as to the caretakers who so amiably unlocked remote churches and monasteries for me.

Foreword

Portugal, cut off from the rest of the continent by the great land mass of Spain and bounded on the west and south by the Atlantic Ocean, is the westernmost country of Europe. Its relatively small area of 34,207 sq miles (88,551 sq kms), falls gradually down from the more mountainous terrain on the frontier to the valleys of the four main rivers, the Tagus, the Douro, the Mondego and the Sado and the flatter country by the sea.

Until the last few years, Portugal was virtually unknown to travellers. Now, more and more people are coming to this country which has an astonishing variety of landscape and of fine architecture as well as unparalleled beaches on its long indented coastline. There are mercifully few motorways, so the motorist, not only should, but must take his time in getting around.

With the exceptions of Lisbon with around a million inhabitants and Oporto with 400,000, the population of almost ten million is mainly concentrated in the north and centre of the country, the Algarve and the Alentejo being far more sparsely populated. Widespread emigration to France and Germany and to a lesser degree to Brazil, has been mostly from the north, the Minho, Tras-os-Montes, Douro and the Beiras. The effects of this can be seen in the prosperity of even remote villages, for the emigrants almost always return to their *terra*, their native soil, with the money they have prudently saved and rebuild their houses.

The Portuguese are kindly and easy going and many old-fashioned values, which have disappeared in other countries, are still preserved. Family life is important, the aged are respected and children take a full part in the life of their parents and siblings.

The country is divided into provinces: from north to south, these are the Minho, highly cultivated and wooded; Tras-os-Montes, literally Over-the-Hills, in the extreme north-eastern corner of the country, is mainly a high plateau where sheep graze; sweet chestnut and walnut trees flourish on the lower slopes as do vines on the steep terraces falling down to the river Douro in the south, from which the grapes for port wine are gathered.

The Douro is the smallest province, surrounding Oporto and much like the Minho in its level of cultivation and numerous villages. It is in this part of the country that there are the most important Iron Age remains as well as a plethora of early Christian churches. The Beiras, Litoral (Coastal), Alta (Upper) and Baixa (Lower), stretch from the Atlantic right across to the Spanish frontier. The Beira Litoral below Oporto, is cut by rivers and waterways and is one of the main rice-growing regions, particularly along the lower reaches of the Mondego below the ancient University city of Coimbra. The Beira Alta and the Beira Baixa are the most mountainous regions of the country, with the Serra da Estrela cutting across from north east to south west, and other lesser ranges. The lower slopes of these mountains are covered with wooded plantations, the summits rocky with the occasional pasturage for sheep, and lakes, some artificial, lighten the austere country and provide irrigation for small plots of fertile land.

The Mondego valley, east of Coimbra, consists of rich arable land and vineyards in the Dão region. The valley of the river Zezere rises to the Cova da Beira, famous for sheep and the main wool producing part of the country. Many of the towns and villages are fortified against the traditional enemy – Spain. The houses are of granite and seem to sink into the bare landscape of the upper reaches.

Estremadura, running up the coast from Lisbon to Leiria and south to Setúbal, is undulating and cultivated, the land nearer to Lisbon supplying most of the fruit and vegetables for the capital. The few ranges of low hills include those on which the Lines of Torres Vedras were erected in the Peninsular War to protect Lisbon, the Serra de Sintra, to the west of the capital and the Serra da Arrabida to the south of the Tagus, which falls down to the river Sado.

Up river from Lisbon lies the Ribatejo, the rich riverine plain with rice fields, market gardens and great pastures on which splendid horses and black fighting bulls roam freely. Santarem, a leading agricultural centre, is the main city of this province. The smaller towns and villages are prosperous and busy and many of the '*campinos*', or herdsmen, still wear their traditional dress of black breeches, white stockings, red waistcoats and stocking caps.

The Alentejo occupies nearly a third of the total land area of the country between the Atlantic Ocean and Spain. The province is flat, with every eminence crowned by a castle-topped whitewashed village or town. Vast wheatfields stretch into the shimmering distance and groves of olive trees and cork oaks provide the only shade. Herds of razor-backed black pigs root around for acorns and provide the delicious fresh and cured pork for which the Alentejo is famous. Low hills go up to the Spanish frontier, along which are remote and isolated fortified villages, some now utterly deserted, as well as the large and prosperous cities of Elvas, Estremoz and Portalegre. Evora is the lovely, unspoilt capital of the Upper Alentejo; Beja, now industrialised, of the Lower. Numerous dams and irrigation projects have rendered the dry land more fertile, as they have in the southernmost province, the Algarve.

The Algarve is now the best known part of Portugal for the visitor. The sandy beaches are endless, clean and safe on the southern coast, the few to the west sometimes getting the full force of the Atlantic. Inland there are many interesting and beautiful places and Faro, the capital, is one of the most fascinating cities in Portugal.

General Information

How to get there

Air

Portugal's national airline TAP, Air Portugal, has daily services to most European capitals from Lisbon, Faro and Oporto. British Airways also flies daily to these cities and several lines fly from British provincial airports and from Gatwick.

Transatlantic flights are operated by TAP and TWA to and from New York, and TAP and Canadian Pacific cover Toronto and Montreal. Most airlines have fly/drive arrangements at reasonable cost, which are worth looking into as it is often impossible to hire a car on arrival in the country. Package tours with hotel and breakfast or half or full board included, are sometimes cheaper than the ordinary return air fare.

Sea

There are now no regular sailings between Lisbon and either the UK or North America. Brittany Ferries run a direct route from Plymouth to Santander in Northern Spain, which is the quickest way to take your own car to Portugal and avoids the long haul down through France and across Spain.

Frontier posts with Spain are open from 07.00 to 01.00. But those at Caia, Vilar Formoso, Vila Verde da Raia and Valença do Minho do not close at all in the summer months or at Christmas and Easter.

Rail

The 'Sud' runs daily from Paris to Lisbon with 2nd class couchettes and 1st class sleepers, though those taking the latter have to change at Irun on the French/Spanish frontier. There is a restaurant car and for those who enjoy leisurely rail travel, the 26 hours in the train are well spent. Some trains take cars from Paris to Lisbon.

Travel within the Country

Air

Regular daily air services connect Lisbon with Oporto and Faro. Some country towns are linked to the capital by small aircraft.

Rail

There is a good railway network over the country. The only express trains are those between Sta Apolonia Station in Lisbon and Oporto, four of which each day take cars for a modest price. Passengers can travel on a different train to that on which their car travels and pick it up when they like at their destination. Trains can be very crowded, so it is wise to buy your 1st or 2nd class ticket in advance and get a reserved place. Cars are also taken on certain trains to and from Guarda, Regua and in the summer to Faro. For passengers the Lisbon/Algarve line starts at Barreiro, on the south side of the river Tagus, reached by ferry from the Sul e Leste Station at Praça do Comercio. There are minor lines from Oporto to Tras-os-Montes which are slow but scenically rewarding.

One of the most picturesque lines is that from Lisbon to Guarda via Abrantes. Shortly after passing the romantic castle of Almourol on an island in the Tagus, the train follows the river for some 40 miles on a single track line cut out of the side of the hills. There are no roads, the slopes are sparsely cultivated, olive trees perch on what look like inaccessibly steep bluffs, rare birds swoop and dive and the colour of the water is changed by the springs which feed it.

Frequent electric trains link Caes do Sodré station in Lisbon, with Estoril, Cascais and the other resorts on the Sunny Coast. Another electric line goes to Sintra from the Rossio Station in Lisbon. It is essential to buy your ticket before starting as, if bought on the train, there is a *very* heavy surcharge. Travellers over 65 will pay half the basic fare on production of their passport or identity card on all trains in Portugal, except at the rush hour on suburban lines.

Roads   Traffic keeps to the right, vehicles entering roads from the right have priority, unless there is a Stop sign at the junction. There are very few motorways. Most roads are well surfaced, but narrow and twisting. The Portuguese are notoriously bad drivers and take appalling risks. In the north there are still bullock-drawn carts and people riding mules and donkeys. Pedestrians walk in the road both in the towns and in the country.

Buses   Bus services cover every part of the country and long distance lines link Lisbon with the Algarve, Oporto and other places. Lisbon, Oporto and Coimbra have bus and tram services and Lisbon also has an underground.

Taxis   Taxis run on meters and are cheap by international standards. The driver has a right to charge for the return journey if taken outside the town boundaries and 20 percent more from 22.00 to 06.00. Taxis are instantly recognised by their green roofs and black bodies.

Car Hire   Avis, Contauto, Hertz, InterRent and most international firms have offices at Lisbon, Faro and Oporto airports, as well as many local firms. It is wise to hire your self-drive car before arrival as there is a great run on these cars in the high season. Visitors bringing their own cars should have a valid British, American or international driving licence, international car insurance (green card), and nationality plates, as well as a luminous triangle for use when a car is immobilised on the highway. Spare parts are available. The Portuguese Automobile Club is the Automovel Clube de Portugal, Rua Rosa Araujo 24–26, 1200 Lisbon. Fuel prices are among the highest in Europe. Seat belts are obligatory in the country, but not in towns.

8

Where to stay

Local tourist offices have lists of hotels and boarding houses in every category. Some of the luxury hotels are superb and the Government sponsored *Pousadas* are often located in converted castles and fine old houses. Accommodation in *Pousadas* is limited to three days in the high season. Prices include all taxes and service charges.

Estalagems are privately run tourist inns and are often located in towns as are *Residencias*, which only serve breakfast. But every town in Portugal has reasonable restaurants. Pensões or boarding houses are very good value, though it is rare to get a private bathroom. The Portuguese are very clean and even in Lisbon and large towns, housewives hang out their wash to dry from struts attached to window sills or balconies, regardless of passers-by, so even the humblest pension is usually clean and neat.

There are good camping sites and youth hostels all over the country, particulars from the tourist offices. There is great freedom of parking for caravans, as there are not too many.

Holiday homes, rented for short periods are almost unknown outside the Algarve, but there form a major business and all the main agents abroad have their correspondents in the Algarve who supply full particulars, arrange for visitors to be met at Faro Airport by a self-drive car, and see there is food in the refrigerator for the first meal. The services of cleaning women, who come in every morning, are included in the rent.

Hotels

Pousadas

Estalagems
Residencias
Pensions

Camping

Holiday Homes

Banks and Currency

Banking hours are from 08.30 to midday and 13.30 to 14.30. Closed on Saturdays. The unit of currency is the escudo, with the dollar sign between the escudo and the centavos. Thus, 105$50 is one hundred and five escudos and fifty centavos. The rate of exchange varies and a better rate is to be had at banks than in hotels or shops. One pound sterling is equal to approximately 130 escudos. Travellers cheques in sterling or dollars are the safest way to carry money. Notes of 5,000$00, 1,000$00, 500$00, 100$00, 50$00 and 20$00 are in circulation as are coins of 25$00, 10$00, 5$00, 2$50, 1$00 and $50.

Churches

There is no state religion in Portugal but the vast majority of the population is Roman Catholic, so there are Catholic churches with Mass on Sundays in every town and village.

The Church of England has churches in Lisbon, Estoril, Oporto, and the Algarve. These are St George's, St Paul's, St James and St Vincent's respectively.

9

The Irish Dominican Order has served the catholic church of Corpo Santo in Lisbon for over 300 years. Masses in English on Sundays and weekdays. On Sundays in St Sebastian's Chapel in Cascais, and in Parede. Various other bodies have churches or meeting places which are listed under *Igreja*, in the telephone directories.

Clubs and Libraries

The Royal British Club, Rua da Estrela 8, 1200 Lisbon, is mainly a lunch club. The American Women of Lisbon have a Club house in Cascais at Avenida de Sintra 3, with meals and various activities. The Anglo-American Library is on the premises, open every morning until midday, except Sundays. The British Institute, Rua Luis Fernandes 3, 1200 Lisbon, has an excellent library and reading room, open daily except Wednesday mornings and the American Library, attached to the US Embassy, at Avenida Duque de Loulé 22-B, 1000 Lisbon, is open every afternoon.

Consulates

The British Consulate is at Rua São Domingos à Lapa 37, 1200 Lisbon, tel. 661191, the US Consulate at Avenida Duque de Loulé, 39, 1000 Lisbon, tel. 570102 and the Canadian at Rua Rosa Araujo, 2–6, 1200 Lisbon, tel. 562547.

Customs

Customs formalities are similar to those in other European countries.

Dress

The sun can be dangerously hot in the summer and it is not safe to be a long time on the beach without a shady hat. When it rains, which is rare in the six summer months, it comes down with tropical intensity and the temperature falls after sunset, so even in the summer it is wise to bring a light coat. (Snow is almost unknown, as are heavy frosts in winter.) Low heeled, comfortable shoes are essential for walking in Lisbon, or any other town or village as pavements are usually made up of mosaics of tiny stones and even in the north, where the paving stones are of granite, they are seldom kept evenly laid. In short, dress for both men and women is much the same as in any other warm southern country.

Etiquette

The Portuguese are a formal people and good manners will get the visitor anywhere. Shake hands with your hairdresser, hotel porter and indeed anyone who has been especially helpful. Visitors always turn round to say a final farewell before disappearing from view. The words '*com licença*', 'allow me', are a great help if for instance you find all the tables occupied in a café, and want to sit in a vacant chair, or have to push past anyone in a crowd.

Festivals and Entertainment

Romarias or religious festivals, are held to honour the local patron
saint in countless towns and villages. The most famous pilgrimage
centre in the whole Iberian peninsula is that of Fatima, 90 miles
north of Lisbon, where huge crowds of pilgrims gather on the 13th
of each month from May to October to commemorate the apparitions of the Virgin to three shepherd children there in 1917.

Romarias

Country fairs are always held in connection with *romarias*, and
most country towns have their regular weekly or monthly market
of fatstock and produce.

The Calouste Gulbenkian Foundation has done much to bring
music and ballet into the provinces, with special festivals held in
different cities during the summer, in addition to the winter and
spring programmes at the headquarters in Lisbon.

Music

The latest films are shown in all cinemas and Portuguese TV relies
heavily on imported programmes.

Cinema

Casinos with roulette, French bank and slot machines are at Estoril
near Lisbon, Alvor, Monte Gordo and Vilamoura in the Algarve,
Figueira da Foz near Coimbra and Espinho and Povoa de Varzim on
the Costa Verde in the north. Visitors must take their passports.

Casinos

Food and Wine

The Portuguese eat food that is in season, as frozen and packaged
food is far more expensive than fresh food. Fish is superb, but dear
apart from fresh sardines, fruit and vegetables excellent when
carefully chosen; all shopkeepers allow customers to feel fruit and
vegetables and even fish. Battery chickens have only started to be
produced recently so most poultry is well flavoured. Beef is apt to
be tough; pork both fresh and in its many smoked forms is
excellent; lamb and mutton have to be chosen with care as they
tend to be scraggy. Every part of Portugal has its local cheese,
usually made from ewe's or goat's milk. The best known are the
Queijo da Serra, from the Estrela mountains, like a softer type of
Brie. Azeitão, from near Setúbal is somewhat similar. *Ilha* or *São
Jorge* is a type of Cheddar from the Azores Islands and is excellent
for cooking. The small *Queijos Frescos* and *Requeijão* made from
goat's milk curds, should be eaten fresh to capture the real flavour
Most produce is considerably cheaper in local markets which are in
every town and village, than in shops or supermarkets.

Some of the best wines in Portugal are purely local, such as
Bussaco in Coimbra, Nabantino in Tomar and Vidigueira in the
Alentejo. But these local wines are gradually becoming available in
Lisbon and other cities and if you are eating in a restaurant with a
wine list, look out for the more unfamiliar names. Dão, Colares,
Azeitão and Lagoa, both red and white, rosés such as Mateus and

Wines

11

the green, slightly petillant wines from the north are on most wine lists. In more modest eating houses ask for the *vinho da casa*, that is the house wine; it is almost always good, either red, *tinto*, or white, *branco*.

Sagres is the best known name in lager and beer and there are other good types of foreign beers.

Port is little drunk in its country of origin, but is available in most places. White port is taken as an aperitif before meals and the heavier reds, tawny, crusted and vintage come in all the famous names. There is a fascinating Port Wine Institute in Lisbon, open from 10.00 to midnight, at Rua S. Pedro de Alcantara 45, where there are 200 varieties to be tasted and where the wine can be bought by the bottle or the case. Madeira is a drier, more sherry-like wine and there is a delicious sweet Muscatel from Setúbal.

Spirits   Portuguese brandy can be very good, as is the local gin. Vodka, and every type of liqueur, is imitated and is very much less expensive than imported spirits. Whisky, however, cannot be imitated and genuine Scotch is around double what it costs in the UK.

Gratuities

Tips are now included in hotel and restaurant bills, but a small five to ten percent is acceptable and wise if you intend to return. Porters expect 10$00 per bag, theatre ushers, cloakroom girls and boot-blacks the same. Men give 20$00 in barbershops and women 20$00 to 50$00 according to the services rendered. Museum custodians receive 20$00 and 50$00 if a party is taken round. Taxi drivers should get 5$00 on short fares, 10$00 on longer ones.

Language

Portuguese is a difficult language to speak or to understand, but easily read by anyone with some knowledge of a Latin language. As the people are kindly and cooperative, it is seldom difficult to get what you want even in a remote pension or shop.

Medical Services

The Portuguese National Health Service has improved greatly of recent years and a reciprocal agreement exists between the British and Portuguese Services, though not every hospital knows this fact. Many doctors and specialists have done post-graduate work in Great Britain or the United States, so English-speaking doctors are not difficult to find. There is a British Hospital with English-speaking nurses and doctors, at Rua Saraiva de Carvalho 49, 1200 Lisbon, tel. 602020, with a daily Out-Patients department, two small wards and several single rooms.

Museums

Normally open from 10.00 to midday and from 14.00 to 17.00 every day except Monday. Entrance fees are around 20$00, free on Saturdays and Sundays. Palaces are closed on Tuesdays.

Offices

These are open from 09.30 or 10.00 to 17.30 or 18.00 with a break for lunch. Post Offices have the same opening hours, with the exception of the main Offices which remain open during lunch.

Passports

No visas are required for holders of British, Irish or USA passports on entering Portugal. But if their stay is longer then 60 days, application for an extension must be made to the relevant department, by the place in which they are staying. Health certificates are not required.

Public Holidays

New Year's Day (January 1), anniversary of the 1974 Revolution (April 25), Labour Day (May 1), National Day (June 10), Corpus Christi (moveable), the Assumption (August 15), First Republic (October 5), All Saints (November 1), Restoration (December 1), Immaculate Conception (December 8), Christmas Day (December 25).

Restaurants

It is rare to find badly cooked food in a restaurant. The best restaurants are very good and much less dear than their counterparts in the UK. There is a wide range of middle priced places with dishes at around 200$00, but the portions are so large that few eat more than one course and it is customary for three people to share two portions of an entrée and of the main course. Cheap restaurants called *tascas*, can be distinguished from taverns by the fact that they have tablecloths and food is not served on marble or plastic-topped tables. The food is rough but well flavoured. Meal times are later than in the UK or USA. Lunch seldom starts before 13.00 to 13.30 and dinner before 20.00.

Cafés and pastrycooks are everywhere and often serve simple meals of ham and eggs or meat pasties or rissoles. Cakes are sweet and rich, sometimes with nuts and eggs incorporated.

Shopping

Opening hours vary greatly; shops in commercial centres are often open all day and on Sundays until 23.00 or midnight. However, many shops still open at 09.00, shut for two hours for lunch, usually from 13.00 to 15.00, though in the north midday to 14.00 is the more usual time and remain open till 19.00. On Saturdays these shops shut at 13.00. The best buys are the local craftsmanship –

basketwork, lace, embroidery, leather, filigree jewellery, copper-
ware, pottery, porcelain, cork, local textiles, carpets, musical instruments, marble and woodwork.

Spas

Portugal is rich in Spas, recommended for a variety of complaints.
These thermal waters are now coming back into fashion and for
certain rheumatic complaints they are unrivalled. The better
known Spas all have good hotels, full of old world charm. The best
for rheumatism are at Caldas da Rainha and the Termas dos Cucos,
with natural hot mud baths, near Torres Vedras, both not far from
Lisbon, and Caldas de Monchique in the Algarve. For digestive
troubles and kidney complaints, Luso and Curia, near Aveiro,
Vidago and Pedras Salgadas in the north, Monfortinho near Castelo Branco and Vimeiro north of Lisbon, are all highly thought of.
There are sulphur baths for asthma and bronchitis at Entre-
os-Rios near Oporto and circulatory troubles are said to be improved at Caldelas near Braga, where the waters have the same
mineral content as those at Bad Kissingen in Bavaria.

Sport

Bathing

Almost every beach in Portugal is wide and sandy. Those in the
Algarve are particularly good with safer swimming than those on
the west coast, where the heavy Atlantic rollers can be a serious
hazard. It is therefore wiser to bathe from a beach with a Guard and
bathing is forbidden when it is considered to be dangerous. The
beaches on the estuary of the Tagus are apt to be polluted. Nude
bathing is not usual and is confined to a few beaches in the Algarve
and on the Costa da Caparica, south of Lisbon.

Bullfighting

The Portuguese bullfight is entirely different from the Spanish
version. The bull is not killed and he is fought by superb horsemen
called *cavaleiros*, on magnificent stallions, which are as highly
trained as polo ponies. The *toureiros*, on foot, first engage the bull
with skilled cape work, before the rider enters the fray and as the
bull charges again and again, places a dart in the thick muscles of
the beast's huge neck. Finally, when the bull is tired, the *cavaleiro*,
who wears 18th century costume, rides out of the ring and the bull
is faced by eight *moços de forcado*, who come in on foot, barehanded, in single file to confront the bull. Their leader goes on
alone, challenging the beast with loud cries and, when the bull
charges, the man throws himself at its head and does a handspring
on its horns while the other men grapple with the bull barehanded,
and subdue it. These *pegas*, as the rites of the *moços* are called,
may have been imported in early times from Greece or Rome, as
they much resemble the dances of the sacred bull to be seen on
Cretan and Etruscan vases.

Finally, a group of oxen is let into the ring and the bull gallops out
with them. Specially brave bulls are kept for breeding, the others

14

are slaughtered for meat. The season lasts from Easter to October. The best fights take place in Lisbon at Campo Pequeno, and in the towns up the Ribatejo where the horses and the bulls are bred.

Portugal has deep sea fishing all the year round and manned fishing boats are easy to hire in the main fishing ports of Cascais, Sesimbra, Ericeira, Peniche and Nazaré, as well as in the lagoons near Aveiro and all the small ports north of Oporto and those in the Algarve. Sea fishing is also extensively practised from the shore and it is usual to see fishermen with their rods on the sea wall beside the Estrada Marginal from Lisbon to Cascais. *Fishing*

The best freshwater fishing for trout and salmon, is in the Minho, Lima and Vouga rivers in the north. Undersea fishing is practised all along the coast, particularly in the lagoons in the Sotavento or eastern end of the Algarve, and in the very deep waters off the Berlenga Islands near Peniche. The *Abrigo para Pescadores*, in an old fort jutting into the sea off Berlenga Grande, has rough accommodation and boats for hire.

There are several famous championship courses in the Algarve, an 18 and nine hole course at Estoril, nine hole at Carregueira near Lisbon and others at Vidago, Vimeiro, Miramar and Espinho near Oporto and in Madeira and the Azores. *Golf*

Sailing is a popular pastime and boats can be hired at many of the beach resorts, as can water-skis and wind-surfers. *Sailing*

Most shooting in Portugal is free to anyone with a gun and a licence, in the short shooting season in the late autumn, but there are areas clearly marked *Regime Florestal*, where no shooting is allowed. Information from the various Tourist Offices. *Shooting*

Tourist Offices

The Portuguese Tourist Board in London is at New Bond Street House, 1/5 New Bond Street, 1st Floor, W1, tel. 01-493 3873. In the United States, 548 Fifth Avenue, New York, NY 10036, tel. (212) 3544403/4/5/6/7; the Palmer House, Suite 500, 17 East Monroe Street, Chicago, tel. (312) 2366603, and 1 Park Plaza, Suite 1305, 3250 Wilshire Boulevard, Los Angeles, tel. (213) 3806459. In Canada, 390 Bay Street, Toronto, Ontario M5H 2Y2, tel. (416) 3648133 and 1801 McGill College Avenue, Suite 1150, Montreal QUE H3A 2N4, tel. (514) 2821264/65/66.

Every town of any size in Portugal has a tourist office with brochures and town plans, often in several languages. Details of local buses and trains as well as of coach trips, are available too. The main Tourist offices in Lisbon are in the Palacio Foz, Praça dos Restauradores, 1000 Lisbon, tel. 367031/2/3/4, and Avenida Antonio Augusto de Aguiar 86, 1000 Lisbon, tel. 575086, and at the Airport.

Castle at Belvner

History and Culture

History

First King

Portugal has not changed its frontiers since Afonso Henriques, son of Henry of Burgundy and Teresa, daughter of the King of Leon and Castille, proclaimed himself King of Portucale in 1139 at Guimarães in the north, though it was not until a century later that the Moors were finally driven out of Faro in the extreme south.

Moors

Iron Age

From the amount of building and artifacts that remain, it is known that Portugal, with the rest of the Iberian Peninsula, was settled in the Iron Age and Celtic periods. The Greeks and the Phoenicians established trading posts on the coasts and the Romans and the Visigoths both left their marks as did the Moors, who invaded from North Africa in the 8th century.

Romans

With the coming of the kingdom, the chief preoccupation was the fear of Spanish aggression and the victory over the Castillians at Aljubarrota in 1385 gave the country two centuries of calm. The first Treaty of Alliance with England was signed in 1373 on the marriage of King John I and Philippa of Lancaster, daughter of John of Gaunt, followed by the Treaty of Windsor in 1386, which is the oldest Treaty in the world to be still in force.

The following century saw Prince Henry the Navigator, third of the six sons of King John and Queen Philippa, planning and preparing the voyages of discovery down the coast of Africa, finally rounding Cape Bojador, beyond which the ancients believed that the sea fell into a bottomless abyss. This prepared the way for Columbus to discover America in 1492, for Vasco da Gama to reach India by sea in 1498, Pedro Alvares Cabral to land in Brazil in 1500 and Magellan to circumnavigate the world between 1519 and 1522. These voyages and discoveries resulted in the Portuguese acquisition of their overseas possessions – Angola, Mozambique and Guinea in Africa, Timor and Macau in the Far East and Brazil. The last named became independent in 1825. Portugal also gained Goa and a large part of India, which went to the British Crown as part of Catherine of Braganza's dowry when she married King Charles II. India annexed Goa in 1961 and the remaining overseas possessions were given their independence in 1975 after the Revolution of 1974, which changed Portugal from being the Corporate State envisaged by Dr Oliveira Salazar, who was in power for almost 40 years, to the present democratically elected President and Government. Macau, an enclave on the Chinese mainland, is now the only Portuguese overseas possession, presumably because China wants it so.

The Discoveries

Portugal Overseas

Portugal underwent a Spanish Domination from 1580 to 1640, when the Braganzas, a cadet branch of the royal family, led an uprising, turned the Spaniards out of the country and assumed the monarchy, which they retained until the Revolution of 1910.

Spanish Domination

The riches that poured into Portugal from Brazil and India in the 16th century and, to a lesser degree, from Africa in the 18th century, enabled the kings and the leading churchmen to indulge in a passion for building, the results of which can be seen today by the fortunate visitor.

Gold from India and Brazil

The country was invaded during the Napoleonic Wars and Wellington, only later to be created a Duke, led British and Portuguese troops to the victorious Battle of Bussaco in 1810. The Civil War between the two brothers, Dom Pedro and Dom Miguel, ended in 1834 in favour of Dom Pedro who became King and an expulsion of monks and nuns from their monasteries and convents followed soon after. In the ensuing decades there was much political instability and religious were gradually allowed to return, though not to their original monasteries which often fell into complete ruin. This instability culminated in the assassination of King Carlos I and his heir in 1908, when they were driving in an open carriage through the streets of Lisbon. He was succeeded by his younger son, Manuel II, who, with his mother, had witnessed the murder of his father and brother. The young Manuel abdicated in 1910 and a Republic was proclaimed.

Peninsular War

King Assassinated

Republic

Partly owing to Portugal entering the war of 1914–18, with the Allies against Germany, there were constant political and econo-

17

Dr Salazar	mic crises. Dr Oliveira Salazar, a Professor of Economics at Coimbra University, was called in, becoming Minister of Finance in 1928 and Head of the Government in 1932. He restored economic stability, kept Portugal out of the Second World War, though allowing Great Britain facilities in the Azores Archipelago, after the Treaty of Windsor had been invoked, and retired after a stroke in 1968.
Revolution	Salazar was succeeded as Prime Minister by Dr Marcelo Caetano, a Professor of Law at Lisbon University. But he was not strong enough to continue the dictatorship which Dr Salazar had exercised and was thrown out at the Revolution of April 25th, 1974. Since then there have been many changes of government and of President, but the country is carrying on and in spite of large-scale inflation, the majority of the population is more prosperous than ever before.
Refugees from Africa	After independence in Portuguese Africa almost a million men, women and children poured into Portugal from Angola and Mozambique. These *retornados*, or 'returned ones' as they were called, were of every colour and level of education, though they all spoke Portuguese. Thus the country had to absorb about a tenth of her whole population. Today only a very small proportion has not been resettled. Among the latter are many of the Timorense who fled that far eastern island when it was taken over by Indonesia. For few of these speak Portuguese and negotiations are taking place through the United Nations, as to their future.

Culture

Religion	Unlike many other southern European countries, Portugal has for long possessed freedom of religious beliefs. There have been Anglican churches in Lisbon, Oporto and Funchal, Madeira, since the 18th century, a Scots Church in Lisbon for at least a hundred years and places of worship of many small sects are to be found in most of the larger cities.
Roman Catholic	Some 90 percent of Portuguese profess to be Roman Catholics and, since the rise of Fatima as a great international shrine of Our Lady, the numbers of those attending Mass have greatly increased. The people in the north are noticeably more devout than those in the south, where parts of the Alentejo and the Algarve are considered to be mission territory.
	The most important artistic manifestations in the country are ecclesiastical or stem from church patronage, as a result of the centuries old adherence to the Catholic faith. Incidentally the term 'convent' can be used for a religious house of either men or women.
Primitive painting	Thus, the fascinating School of Portuguese Primitive painting is almost entirely religious in character.

18

The late, highly decorated Gothic style is known as Manueline, after King Manuel I, whose reign of 26 years from 1495 to 1521 saw the opening of the sea routes to Brazil and the Indies. It is almost entirely ecclesiastical, though it derives its inspiration from the Discoveries, using coral, seaweed, ropes, anchors and the armillery sphere, carved in stone as if it were plaster.

The Manueline melted into the Renaissance and as trade with the *Renaissance* Orient increased, Chinese influence was displayed in pottery, china and furniture. The great artistic impulses of Europe reached Portugal considerably later than central Europe and the Baroque *Baroque* and Rococo, with the completely individual twist given to these manifestations by the Portuguese, went on right into the last century.

Although *saudade*, 'yearning', is a characteristic Portuguese word, and the *fados*, the love-sick songs, which are supposed to be so typical of the country, are melancholy, the Portuguese are not a sad or violent race. Their religion, unlike that of the Spaniards, is cheerful and this is particularly shown in the gaiety of Portuguese Baroque. Angels skitter up and down twisted columns, great pictorial panels of glazed blue and white tiles (*azulejos*) line both *Azulejos* the interiors and exteriors of churches. In many places houses are also decorated with this fascinating form of art which is peculiar to Portugal. Dutch and Arabic tiles are much smaller and patterned rather than representative.

There is an abundance of clay for both porcelain and pottery in the *China* country. Lovely porcelain is made at the Vista Alegre works near Aveiro in the Beira Litoral and at Coimbra. The latter city is also a great centre for fine pottery which has been produced there for centuries. The Barcelos cocks in all colours and all sizes are well known as are the vivid glazed green leaf-shaped plates and dishes from Caldas da Rainha. Other types of pottery come from Alcobaça, Mafra, the Alentejo, where small painted figurines are made and the Algarve, with traditional Greek and Roman forms of water pots and jugs still being produced.

Other crafts are basket work of all types, carved wooden ox yokes *Crafts* and household utensils, copper and ironwork and the filigree jewellery made of silver wire and then gold plated.

Lace and embroidery are also traditional crafts. The best-known *Lace and* embroidery comes from Viana do Castelo in the north, with motifs *Embroidery* of hearts and flowers and from Madeira, the Portuguese island in the Atlantic. Arraiolas specialises in hand embroidered wool carpets in many old and modern designs and Castelo Branco is noted for silk embroidered bedspreads and hangings. Fine tapestries come from Portalegre and linen is hand-woven in the north where flax is grown.

The two Portuguese writers whose names are widely known *Literature* abroad are Camões, who wrote the epic poem the *Lusiads* in 1572, commemorating the Discoveries, which has often been translated into English, as well as some lovely sonnets, and Eça de Queiroz, the late Victorian novelist. His books, all of which have been translated into English, are realistic and vividly show the life of the professional classes of his period in Portugal. Other famous writers are the 16th century Gil Vicente who wrote plays, Almeida Garrett who introduced the Romantic movement into Portugal in the last century and, in this century, Fernando Pessoa, Aquilino Ribeiro, Miguel Torga, Ferreira de Castro, Fernando Namora, Joaquim Paço d'Arcos and Luis Sttau Monteiro.

Mills

Windmills, the sails of coarse cotton or linen, reset by the farmer when the whine of the clay whistles on the struts changes and so tells him that the wind has altered, still stand on many hills, particularly in the south and watermills are on the banks of some northern rivers. The old tidal mills up the Tagus, have mostly disappeared as have the *fragatas*, the specially constructed boats which ferried goods across the Tagus before the bridge over the river was built some 20 years ago.

Misericordias

Queen Leonor founded the first Misericordias, or Hospitals of Mercy, in the 15th century and these have always been managed by lay bodies of local people. The chapels attached to the old buildings are often of exceptional interest, containing fine paintings and furnishings. Now that modern hospitals have been built all over the country, the former Misericordias are often used as homes for old people, who are thus able to go on living in their own towns or villages.

Music

The Portuguese are a musical people and sing as they go about their work. Dancing at the country fairs and *romarias* is accompanied by song and almost every town or village of any size has a band. There are no world famous composers, though there were known writers of ecclesiastical music in the 17th and 18th centuries.

Fado

However, unique to Portugal, is the *Fado*. This is a plaintive ballad, wailed rather than sung, of unrequited love, passion or despair. The *Fadista*, man or woman, wears black in memory of Maria Severa, the most famous and notorious of the early 19th century singers, who died young. The song is accompanied by two guitarists, the audience listens in complete silence and then when the last strange gutteral note is wrung from the tense body of the singer, the response is wildly enthusiastic. Amalia Rodrigues is still the most famous *Fadista* today and her recordings show something of the attraction of this unusual form of art.

Fados can be heard in Lisbon in special restaurants and cafés, though the performance seldom starts before 22.00 or 23.00. Coimbra, the University town, is another centre, with the students singing together rather than solo as in Lisbon.

20

After the flowering of primitive painting in the 15th century, with *Painting*
the great retable of São Vicente by Nuno Gonçalves in the Lisbon
Art Museum as its apotheosis, and the work of Frei Carlos in Evora,
there were few painters of note. Josefa of Obidos in the 17th
century developed a characteristic countryfied style of her own.
Then, at the end of the 18th and the beginning of the 19th centuries,
Domingos Antonio Sequeira showed by his work that he was a
really great painter of portraits, family groups and allegorical
subjects. He also designed the splendid gold-plated table service
which a grateful Portuguese government presented to the Duke of
Wellington after the Peninsular War. This is on show in Apsley
House in London.

Towards the end of the last century, the leading painter was
Columbano Bordalo Pinheiro, whose admirable portraits can be
seen in the Contemporary Art Museum in Lisbon. A little later there
was Almada Negreiros while the contemporary painter Vieira da
Silva, who became a French national, is widely known for her
abstracts.

Possibly owing to the wealth of stone and marble to be found in the *Sculpture*
country, there are many remarkable sculptures in Portugal, beginning with the unique Iron Age idol, the Colossus of Pedralva, in
Guimarães. The Gothic tombs in Coimbra, Lisbon Cathedral and
the 14th century sarcophagus of D. Pedro and Inez at Alcobaça, are
memorable as are the carved stone retables in many northern
churches. Machado de Castro, in the 18th century, produced the
great bronze equestrian statue of King José I in Lisbon's waterfront
square and a host of delightful polychrome wood and terracotta
figures of the country people of his time, as well as of saints. In the
last century, Soares dos Reis was the leading sculptor and his work
can be seen in the museum that bears his name in Oporto.

Domestic building used to vary widely from province to province, *Secular*
but now the country builder seems to have lost the instinctive *Building*
feeling for harmonious proportion which marked the work of his
forebears. However, in the Algarve, the houses are still low and
whitewashed with fantastic chimneys; in the Alentejo, the chimneys get wider and the walls are of an even more dazzling white.
Further north the cottages are constructed of granite blocks which
make the villages sink into the landscape. Oporto is a granite city,
whereas Lisbon's houses and apartment blocks are colour-washed
in every conceivable shade.

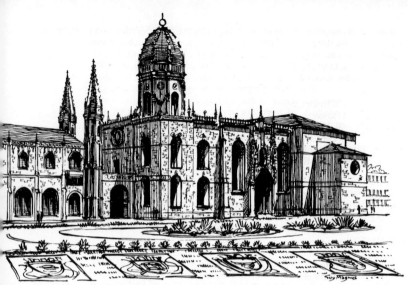
Jeronimos Monastery

Lisbon

The capital of Portugal, with around a million inhabitants, is spread in a wide semi-circle on a number of hills on the banks of the river Tagus. The Tagus is a great river by the time it reaches Lisbon and the Atlantic ocean; since the Greeks traded along the coasts of the Iberian peninsula it has been a lifeline for Lisbon.

It is now believed that the Phoenicians formed a trading settlement here and then the Romans arrived, fortified the hill on which St George's castle now stands and left traces of their occupation all over the country. They gave Lisbon the name of *Felicita Julia*, built roads out of the city and municipal buildings within it. After the Romans withdrew from the peninsula, the Visigoths strengthened the fortifications and after conversion to Christianity, built the first cathedral below the Castle hill.

Next the Moors poured in from Spain and called the city '*Olissibona*', adorning it with buildings, none of which now remains, though traces of the Moorish domination are to be found in place names. These mostly begin with 'Al', not only in Lisbon itself, such as Alcantara, one of the valleys leading to the river, and Alfama, still largely a medieval part of the city, but all over the southern part of the country. The Moors tolerated the Christians, but in 1147 ships with English, German and Flemish Crusaders, who were sailing to the Holy Land, were driven ashore near Oporto by a great storm. The first King of Portugal, Afonso Henriques, who had only secured possession of the northern part of the country, persuaded the men to sail on south and drive the Moors out of Lisbon.

By the mid-13th century the court was settled in Lisbon and then, as now, the Rossio was the centre of the city. It is a fine square with the National Theatre on the north side and surrounded by the formal 18th century houses which the Marques of Pombal, then Prime Minister, built after the great earthquake of 1755. The streets leading from the Rossio to the riverside arcaded square of the Praça do Comercio are all designed on a grid pattern with these beautiful façades on either side – an early example of town planning. The Rua do Ouro, as its name implies, was the goldsmiths' street, the Rua da Prata, the silversmiths', and the Rua Augusta leads down to a triumphal arch giving on to the Praça do Comercio. These streets are lined with banks and good shops, for it is the original commercial section of the city, though there are excellent shops and shopping centres in all the residential parts around the Parque Eduardo VII, at the top of the Avenida da Liberdade, and in the apartment blocks on the way to the airport.

Rossio

In the centre of the Praça do Comercio is the great equestrian bronze statue of Dom José I designed by Machado de Castro. The King, in a breastplate and plumed helmet, astride a splendid horse, has now weathered to a lovely green. Long ago, when the statue was still bronze coloured, the great space was named Black Horse Square by English visitors; and before the assassination of King Carlos I and his elder son in 1908 at the north-west corner of this square in front of the General Post Office, it was called Terreiro do Paço, Palace Yard, as the Royal palace was here up to the 18th century and Catherine of Braganza sailed from this spot to England for her marriage to Charles II.

Praça do Comercio

As has been indicated already, Lisbon is essentially an 18th century city, for the great earthquake and the tidal wave which followed it, destroyed the whole of the lower part of the town. However, the Castle which rises on a hill to the east and the Cathedral below it, still stand, as do many 17th century houses in the Alfama district around the Cathedral. Another early part is the Bairro Alto, on a hill to the west of the Avenida da Liberdade.

Architecture

Lovers of *art nouveau*, will delight in the number of apartment houses and even shop fronts built in the first 20 to 30 years of this century, which are to be found all over the city. The large new office blocks and apartments of the last 35 years have a dignity which you do not find in many other countries, for the door and window surrounds are all of stone or marble and the facades are colour-washed in pastel tones of pink, blue, green or cream, and there are pots of geraniums and other flowering plants on every balcony.

23

<table>
<tr><td>

Public
Transport

</td><td>

Buses and trams run all over Lisbon and are very reasonable in price. Books of 20 tickets, at half the price charged on the vehicle, can be bought outside Cais do Sodré Station and other terminals. The underground has a flat fare rate.

</td></tr>
</table>

Castle

The much-restored St George's castle can be reached either by a bus which starts in the Rossio, a taxi, or by walking uphill past the cathedral. There is no entrance fee and the visitor reaches a wide battlemented grassed space with fine old trees. The view is superb over the centre of the city, with the Rossio and the Praça do Comercio below, the great river which widens above Lisbon into what is called the 'Sea of Straw' and from the top of any of the castle towers, the Sintra hills and the suspension bridge, one of the longest in Europe, thrown across the Tagus in the middle distance.

Wandering around the castle lawns are flocks of white birds – ducks, geese, swans and turkeys; stone benches are provided and tables for picnics. There is also an excellent and expensive restaurant serving lunches and teas – the Casa do Leão.

Between the inner and the outer walls of the castle, there is a largely medieval village with narrow lanes winding between houses, still lived in by local artisans. In the centre is a charming, formal square with benches shaded by plane trees and the church of the Holy Cross at one side. In this square at number 5, Michel's is a luxury French restaurant.

Cathedral

In Portugal, a cathedral is called the Sé (like the See of a bishopric in England), and if a visitor asks for directions to get to the cathedral, he will not be understood. The Lisbon Sé was begun in 1150 and much restored through the centuries. The interior is noble and the renaissance chancel, with a lovely 18th century organ at one side, has not been altered. The chapels behind the high altar contain splendid Gothic tombs, including one of a woman reading a book with two dogs fighting at her feet. Beyond these are the somewhat derelict cloisters with a fine 13th century iron screen to one of the chapels. The font in the cathedral is that in which St Anthony of Padua was baptised in 1195, and it is nice to think of the babies of the parish being christened in the same stone basin. The saint was born in a house opposite the main door of the cathedral and later on a small Italianate-looking church, Santo Antonio da Sé, was built over the spot.

Further up the hill from the cathedral, a public garden to the right gives a bird's eye view of the roofs and narrow alleyways of the Alfama district, which is well worth exploring on foot, with its medieval houses and glimpses of little gardens through grilled apertures set in high walls.

Espirito
Santo
Foundation

The way up goes on to the Fundação Ricardo Espirito Santo Silva. This is a museum and school of the decorative arts in which young men and women are trained in many rare handicrafts, such as

24

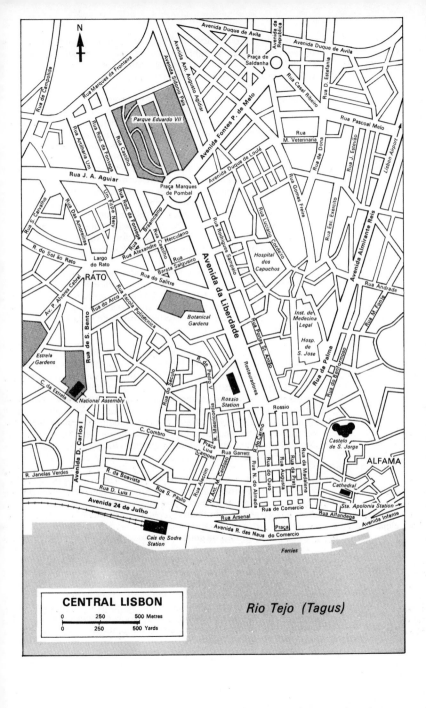

CENTRAL LISBON

0   250   500 Metres
0   250   500 Yards

Rio Tejo (Tagus)

book binding, the application of gold leaf, repairing antique carpets, wood carving, ormulu, sculpture and cabinet making to such a high degree of perfection that the copies of 18th century furniture are all marked with a special cipher to show that they are not genuine, and cannot therefore be sold as antiques by unscrupulous dealers. There are over 20 workshops, each devoted to a different aspect of the decorative arts and this remarkable foundation also runs a course for interior decorators, thus keeping alive the long Portuguese tradition of fine craftsmanship.

Summer Festivities

It is in and around this old part of Lisbon, stretching down from the castle to the wide riverside highway, that the local people make merry on the nights of the feast days of the three patrons of Lisbon, St Anthony on June 12th/13th, St John on the 23rd/24th and St Peter on the 28th/29th. Strings of coloured paper hang across the streets, young people dance to the wild music of the local bands and dances are held in all the covered markets of Lisbon when the fun goes on all night. Little booths sell sizzling fresh sardines, grilled over charcoal and glasses of strong red wine.

Flea Market

On the hill up river, to the east of the castle, behind the great Italianate church of São Vicente, Lisbon's Flea Market, Feira da Ladra, is held every Tuesday and Saturday in the Campo de Sta Clara, but it is now rare to find a bargain there, as it is in the better antique shops in the Rua do Alecrim, the Rua da Escola Politécnica and the Rua de São Bento.

Braganza Pantheon

Off the cloisters at the side of the São Vicente church, is the Braganza Pantheon with the stone coffins of all the later Kings and Queens of Portugal; King John IV who died in 1656, Queen Catherine of Braganza, widow of King Charles II of England who spent the 23 years of her widowhood in Lisbon, and successive royalty through to the last King of Portugal, Manuel II. At one time the coffins had glass tops so that the embalmed bodies could be seen, but this is no longer the case. The latest remains are those of King Carol of Rumania and Madame Lupescu who, on their marriage, became Princess Helene.

Station

Madre de Deus

Tile Museum

Up river, past the pink-washed Victorian station of Sta Apolonia from where the international trains and those for the north of Portugal start, are the church and convent of Madre de Deus. The church is a riot of golden baroque woodwork above huge blue and white *azulejo* panels, and fine canvases. The sacristy, a small jewelled box, should be seen. At the west end of the church, entry can be obtained to the nuns' choir with more good canvases surrounded by baroque woodwork on the walls and ceiling, and to the Tile Museum, Museu do Azulejo. Highly glazed tiles are a unique and very decorative feature of Portuguese architecture. Many houses are entirely covered with either patterned or coloured tiles and shops often have the symbols of their trade depicted in tiles on their shop fronts; such as screws, nails and various tools on an ironmonger's, or joints of meat outside a butcher's. In some 18th century houses, the garden façades are covered with tiled pictures representing trees and foliage reaching right up to the eaves and the majority of old churches are lined, either with blue and white pictorial panels of scriptural subjects, or with what are called 'carpet' tiles, that is, patterned tiles within a surround which, when placed with others on a wall look almost as if they were hanging Persian carpets.

This museum has some unusual early tiled panels, one with two parrots on either side of a huge pot of flowers, dated 1640, and another 50 years later, reproducing strange animals with a cat and a mouse in the corner. There are also examples of the famous *singerie* designs, with monkeys dressed as human beings in set scenes, driving coaches, eating picnics in the country and engaged in other diversions.

North of the Rossio, past the fantastic Moorish-Manueline railway station for local trains to Sintra and the west coast up to Obidos and Leiria, is the Restauradores. This square surrounds an obelisk commemorating the Restoration of 1640, when the detested Spanish yoke of 60 years was overthrown. Underneath is a three-storeyed car park. On the western side, in the 18th century Palacio Foz, is the main tourist office. *Station*

Restauradores

At the side of the square, a funicular tram leads up to São Roque and on the other side one goes to the Campo de Santa Ana. There is another semi-funicular tram in Lisbon, called the Bica, which goes from the Rua de São Paulo to near the top of the Chiado or Rua Garrett, the Bond Street of Lisbon. *Funiculars*

Perhaps the strangest are the lifts springing up from the Rua do Ouro to a metalled bridge leading to the Largo do Carmo. These two large lifts holding around 50 people are worked on the counter-balance system and are enclosed in a Gothic iron fantasy, believed to have been designed by Eiffel whom, it is known, built the great railway bridge of Dona Maria Pia across the Douro in Oporto.

The Avenida da Liberdade is divided by shady gardens, under which the cafés put out tables and chairs in the summer. At the top stands a statue of the Marques de Pombal who, as mentioned, re-planned the building of the city of Lisbon after the great earthquake of 1755. Behind the statue lies the Parque Eduardo VII, a large park with a building for meetings and congresses, and at the top the fascinating Cool House and Hot House. But do not think that these two lovely horticultural collections resemble in any way the hothouses or greenhouses in English parks and gardens. The *Estufa Fria*, or Cool House, over an acre in area, is entirely covered with green slats, giving a curious underwater effect to the delicious air scented by a thousand flowering shrubs, plants and even trees. The slats keep out the sun and yet allow the air to circulate. Narrow streams with water lilies and other aquatic plants, meander by the *Avenida da Liberdade*

Parque Eduardo VII

Cool House

paths and ultimately lead to the *Estufa Quente*, or Hot House, enclosed in a smaller area beyond, by which is a covered hall where concerts are often given in the summer.

Also in this part of Lisbon, some half mile to the north, the Fundação Calouste Gulbenkian is on the Avenida de Berna. Purpose-built, in a superbly landscaped park, the outside of the long, low building has an unfortunate resemblance to an underground train, but the interior could not have been better designed. There are two concert halls, a hall for lectures, an excellent library, two galleries for temporary exhibitions and, most important of all, the museum containing the marvellous collection of art and artifacts collected by the oil millionaire. He stayed in Lisbon for the last years of his life, after escaping from Paris where he then lived, at the beginning of the Second World War.

Gulbenkian, one of the last of the great private collectors, started his passionate interest in the possession of beautiful objects by buying ancient coins in the markets of Constantinople when he was a boy. So the first galleries contain exquisite examples of Greek and Roman coins. There are also wonderful Persian carpets, early Persian glass and sculpture.

The European section contains not only porcelain and furniture, the latter largely of the *Régence* period, but stunning paintings, many of which Gulbenkian bought out of the Hermitage Museum in what was then Petrograd, when the new State of Russia was urgently in need of foreign exchange in the 1920s. Among these pictures from the Hermitage, is the world-famous full-length painting by Rembrandt of his sister-in-law Helène Fourment, standing in a black satin dress with a delicious smile on her face. There is a room full of Guardis, wonderful paintings by La Tour and other canvases showing, contrary to popular belief, that Gulbenkian had a most individual taste and cannot have been dependent only on the advice of experts.

There are also superb 18th century French terracotta busts, a marvellous heroic bronze of Turenne, bronze *animaliers* by Barye and a specially lighted oval room with a collection of Lalique *art nouveau* jewels and ornaments, showing the great imagination and superb craftsmanship of this Frenchman who was working at the beginning of the century.

In the winter and spring, there are special music and ballet festivals lasting for several weeks. The tickets for these concerts and performances are exceedingly moderate in price, owing to the huge endowment that Mr Gulbenkian left for the whole work of his Foundation, which not only covers the arts, but also does a great deal to encourage the experimental theatre, research, education, health and various activities both in Portugal and other countries. Incidentally, the cafeteria is good and reasonable and there are several restaurants opposite the Foundation, including the *Gondo-*

28

la with superb Italian food.

The zoo, Jardim Zoologico, is in beautiful gardens, with superb trees, formal rose beds and stone pools of water. In this lovely setting the animals, in very ample enclosures, look well and happy, for the warm climate of Portugal suits them and only the Polar bears look a little at a loss. *Zoo*

The City of Lisbon Museum is installed in the 18th century Palacio Pimenta at the end of Campo Grande. There are charming early-Victorian canvases and prints of the capital, as well as models. *Museu da Cidade*

Beyond Campo Grande, in Lumiar, the Costume Museum, Museu de Traje, is arranged in another 18th century palace, formerly belonging to the Palmela family. There is a small collection of clothing as well as dolls' houses, miniature furniture and dolls and their clothing. There is a good restaurant and the whole is set in formal gardens. *Costume Museum*

To the west of the Rossio, the Rua do Carmo leads steeply up to the bottom of the Rua Garrett, or Chiado as it is usually called, for many of Lisbon's streets and squares have nicknames. This is the main shopping centre of Lisbon, with elegant shops and good stores. *Rua Garrett*

Nearby are two of the best restaurants in Lisbon. *Tavares*, Rua da Misericordia 37, in a delightful Edwardian setting and the *Aviz*, Rua Serpa Pinto 12-B, smaller, with perfect service and uniquely elegant wash-rooms. *Caravela*, Rua Paiva Andrade, serves light lunches. Go there around 17.30 to see the smart Lisbonians having tea. *Belcanto* in the Largo de S. Carlos by the Opera House is not cheap and is also smart.

However the *Cervejaria da Trindade* at Rua Nova da Trindade 20-B and the *Trindade* at number 10 in the same street both serve good food at very moderate prices as does the *Snack Bar Camões* at 45 Praça Luis de Camões at the top of the Chiado; from here the Rua da Misericordia leads up to the Largo de São Roque in which is the late 16th century church of the same name. The last chapel on the left, that of St John the Baptist, was built by King John V and was constructed in Rome and sent to Lisbon by sea. The agate, lapis lazuli, alabaster, mosaic and rare marbles of which it is built are magnificent in a curiously muted way. In the same aisle, the Cornish nobleman, Sir Francis Tregian, of the famous family of madrigal composers, is buried upright with a long inscription on the tomb relating to his imprisonment for his religion under Queen Elizabeth I, and the 20 years he spent in Portugal where he was regarded as a saint. *São Roque*

Next to the church, and entered through it, is a small museum of ecclesiastical vessels, fine goldsmiths work and superb embroidered vestments. *Religious Art Museum*

Basilica da Estrela	In the big, domed Estrela Basilica, the chief interest to visitors lies in the enormous 18th century Christmas crib by the sculptor Machado de Castro, which is in a great glass case, the size of a small room. The crib, which is reached through the sacristy, is filled with terracotta figures set against scenic hills and paths. These figures are depicted going about their ordinary life, working, cooking, drawing water from the fountain, drinking and even playing cards and are set around a central scene of the Holy Family, most beautifully modelled and painted.
English Cemetery	Nearby is the English cemetery, with beautiful flowering shrubs and tall trees, surrounding the Anglican church of St George. Henry Fielding, the great 18th century novelist, was buried here.
Art Museum	In this part of the town, but nearer the river, is Lisbon's Art Museum, Museu de Arte Antiga. It has a small but fine collection of paintings, porcelain, sculpture, the silver table service made by the French Germain brothers for King John V, and the early 16th century church monstrance fashioned from the first gold to come to Portugal from the Orient. It is a marvellous piece of work, with the Apostles in coloured enamelled cloaks, kneeling round, the soles of their little pink feet giving a charming touch of simplicity to the sophistication of the goldsmiths work surrounding them.

The most famous picture in the collection, is the polyptych of São Vicente by Nuno Gonçalves, a 15th century composition of all the people of Lisbon surrounding the King and his Queen and two figures of St Vincent, patron of the city. Among the crowd are Prince Henry the Navigator in a great black hat, a group of Cistercians from Alcobaça, clerics in strange headgear and a motley group of highly individual faces looking over the heads of the central figures. Similar faces are to be seen in the streets of Lisbon today, for in spite of continual intermarriage with all the races in the formerly enormous Empire, the basic physiognomy of the Portuguese has, as seen in this impressive picture, changed little over the centuries.

Coach Museum	The Coach Museum, Museu dos Coches, at Belem, is the finest in the world, with the great collection of vehicles standing in two long lines down an 18th century riding school. The earliest is late 16th century and there are examples right through to the middle of the Victorian period. At the end of the long gallery, stand three golden baroque coaches with enormous wheels, which brought the Portuguese Ambassador and his suite from Rome in 1716. The later coaches are beautifully painted and there are charming little pony chaises, which were used in the last century by the princesses for driving round the Royal parks. Round the walls hang harnesses and liveries, all kept in perfect condition.
Jeronimos Church ♦	A short way to the west, is one of the most original churches of the world. Begun in 1502, the Jeronimos epitomises the violent excitement which the Portuguese felt at the time of the Discoveries.

Vasco da Gama had charted the sea route to the Indies; Pedro Cabral and Bartolomeu Dias had reached Brazil and here, in stone, imagination runs riot into a wild decoration of ropes, anchors, sea-beasts, coral and astronomical instruments. This is particularly so in the great double cloister behind the church, and in the high doorway overlooking the Tagus, which then came much nearer the building than it does today.

The effect in the interior of the church, is of a vast space with six great octagonal columns, each closely covered with ornate carvings, holding up the enormously high fan tracery of the roof. The wide transept is unsupported and in the later Renaissance chancel are royal tombs strangely placed on the backs of elephants, each animal being slightly different to the others.

In the same building as the rather disorganised Ethnological Museum, at the side of Jeronimos, the Naval Museum, Museu da Marinha, is beautifully arranged, with models of ships as well as the State Barge and other craft. Queen Elizabeth II and Prince Philip were rowed ashore in this Barge from the Royal Yacht 'Britannia' which was anchored in the Tagus on the occasion of the state visit to Portugal in 1957.

Naval Museum

At right angles to the entrance to the Naval Museum, there is a Planetarium built by the Gulbenkian Foundation. The times of shows vary, and are announced on a board outside.

Planetarium

Standing out on the hill behind the Coach Museum, the Ajuda Palace is the epitome of early-Victorian royal splendour. The entrance is 50$00, more than for any of the other palaces or museums, but it is worth it. The reception rooms are lined with splendid tapestries and portraits of royal personages. One room is filled with furniture made of Saxe porcelain which was a wedding present to Queen Maria Pia in 1861 from the King of Saxony. Another room houses enchanting bird cages, made in architectural form.

Ajuda Palace

The Manueline Torre de Belem, rises from the waters of the Tagus to mark the place from which many of the navigators, including Vasco da Gama, sailed on their memorable voyages.

Belem Tower

Nearby the modern monument to the Discoveries faces the river. It is a noble piece of sculpture with Henry the Navigator leading the men of the discoveries up towards the sea and the sky. On the open ground below, a mosaic star-shaped compass shows the lands and seas that were discovered owing to the Navigator.

Monument to Discoveries

In the same area, the museum of the Folk Art of Portugal shows the fast-disappearing country arts and artifacts, including amusing, painted covered carts from the Alentejo.

Folk Art Museum

There are two botanical gardens in Lisbon, one at Belem to the

Botanical Gardens	right of the Monastery, below the Ajuda Palace, with tropical trees and flora, mainly from Brazil, Angola and Mozambique. The other botanical garden lies down the side of the hill between the Rua Escola Politecnica and the Avenida da Liberdade in the centre of Lisbon, and is also a repository of rare trees and plants.
Accomodation	There are several new hotels in Lisbon including the luxury *Sheraton*, Rua Latino Coelho; *Altis*, Rua Castilho, and *Alfa*, Avenida Columbano Bordalo Pinheiro. The rather older *Ritz* in the Rua Rodrigo de Fonseca, overlooking the park, has an excellent restaurant and the *Tivoli* on the Avenida da Liberdade an outstanding top floor grillroom. Round the corner, the four star *Tivoli Jardim* is under the same management and has ample parking space. Other recommended hotels in the four star category are the *Diplomatico*, Rua Castilho; *Fenix*, Praça Marques de Pombal; *Florida* nearby in the Rua Duque de Palmela and the very large, modern *Penta*, Avenida dos Combatentes, ten minutes from the centre of town.

Three star hotels include the *Dom Carlos* and *Embaixador*, both in Avenida Duque de Loulé near the US Embassy; *Eduardo VII*, Avenida Fontes Pereira de Melo; *Jorge V*, Rua Mouzinho da Silveira; *Britania*, Rua Rodrigues de Sampaio and the *Presidente*, Rua Alexandre Herculano, all near the Avenida da Liberdade. The *Miraparque*, Avenida Sidonio Pais has two good Residencias adjoining. *D. Manuel*, *Principe* and *Reno* are all near each other in Avenida Duque d'Avila, not far from the Gulbenkian Foundation. The *Flamingo* is a smaller friendly hotel on Rua Castilho, in which street are also several reasonable pensions.

Estalagems, Residencias, Albergarias and Pensions, mostly serving only breakfast, are all over the city. The best known are *York House* with a restaurant, in a former convent at Rua das Janelas Verdes near the Art Museum; *Senhora do Monte* near the castle; *America*, Rua Tomas Ribeiro; *Imperador*, Avenida 5 de Outubro; *Canada*, Avenida Defensores de Chaves; *Nazareth* and *Mansão Santa Rita*, both in Avenida Antonio Augusto de Aguiar.

Restaurants	The leading luxury restaurants have been mentioned, but there is an endless number of more moderate places, many near the Restauradores at the bottom of the Avenida da Liberdade; *Arameiro* and *Bomjardim* in the Travessa de Santo Antão both serve chicken and suckling pig spit roasted. *Solmar*, Rua Portas de Santo Antão, is more expensive and specialises in seafood, as do many other restaurants in the same street, including the luxury *Gambrinus*.

One of the most agreeable of the cheaper places is *Atinel*, on the Doca dos Cacilheiros, by the ferries at the south-east corner of the Praça do Comercio, with picture windows right on to the Tagus. The Leão d'Ouro behind the Rossio in Rua 1 de Dezembro is one of the oldest restaurants with a famous café. Near Caes de Sodre, the station for electric trains to Estoril and Cascais, the *Porto de*

Jeronimos Church, Lisbon

View over the Tagus from St George's Castle, Lisbon

Beach near Albufeira

Praça do Comercio, Lisbon

Sintra

Hotel Palacio of Seteais

*Village house with typical
Algarve chimney*

Village church near Faro

Houses at Sintra

Abrigo, Rua dos Remolares, is the now smart *tasca* or cheap eating house. Try their crab or duck with rice and olives. There are many other reasonable places around this part of town.

Nearer to Praça Duque de Saldanha, not far from the top of the Avenida da Liberdade, *Forno da Brites* and *Antonio's* are in Rua Tomas Ribeiro; *Mimo*, Avenida Duque d'Avila, and *Colombo*, on Avenida da Republica is near *Galeto*, a well-known snack bar. There are not many self-service places in Lisbon. The best are *Noite e Dia*, Avenida Duque de Loulé and *Sir*, Rua Braamcamp.

Fado places and night clubs come and go. The in-spot for Fados is now *Senhor Vinho*, Rua das Praças. Other well-known Fado restaurants are *A Severa* and *Lisboa a Noite*, both in the Rua das Gaveas; *A Cesaria*, Rua Gilberto Rola; *Mesquita*, Rua Diario de Noticias and *Machado*, Rua do Norte. But it must be remembered that the singing seldom gets going before 23.00.

Fado

Stones, Rua do Olival, is the smartest and most respectable of the night clubs. Others are *O Porão da Nau*, Rua Pinheiro Chagas; *Ti Marciano*, Rua dos Prazeres; *Clube 56*, Rua da Esperança and *Bananas* in Alcantara. There is usually a minimum charge. Bars are apt to be expensive and exclusive as anyone can get a drink in a café or pastry cook's at any time of day.

Night Clubs

Portuguese craftsmen are usually excellent and handmade goods considerably cheaper than in the UK or USA. Specially recommended are glazed tiles from *Viuva Lamego*, Largo do Intendente and *Constancia*, Rua S. Domingos a Lapa; regional pottery at *Grandella's* Department Store and *Festival*, both in Rua do Ouro; and superb porcelain and glass from *Vista Alegre* at the top of the Chiado. Wicker and basket work at *Grandes Armazens das Ilhas*, Rua São Bento; embroidered linens from *Casa Regional da Ilha Verde*, Rua Paiva de Andrade; handbags and leather goods from specialist shops in the Rua do Carmo and Rua Augusta. Handmade shoes from *Helio*, *Orion* and *Mabel* in the Chiado who also stock elegant readymades. Real jewels are often cheaper than in the UK and goldsmiths are all over the city. The best for antique jewels as well as for mending damaged pieces are *Antonio da Silva*, Praça Luis de Camões and *Barreto & Gonçalves*, Rua das Portas de Santo Antão. The *Casa Batalha*, Rua Nova da Almada, founded in 1635, is Lisbon's oldest shop, sells lovely costume jewellery and has skilful repairers. The antique shops down the Ruas Escola Politecnica, São Bento and Santa Marta are dear.

Shopping

Portuguese women are proud of their well-dressed hair, so there are plenty of good hairdressers. *Bruna*, Largo de S. Carlos is the best known and *Tabot*, Avenida Antonio Augisto Aguiar is also good. Spectacles are mended or replaced in a matter of hours and films are also developed rapidly. The *Centro de Turismo e Artesanato*, Rua Castilho 61, not only specialises in regional goods but also despatches goods abroad even if not bought at the shop.

Cascais

Environs of Lisbon

Estoril

The best known of the resorts on the estuary of the Tagus, Estoril is half an hour's drive from Lisbon along the Estrada Marginal. Frequent electric trains from Caes do Sodre station in the capital, take the same time. On the way, there are several other beaches with restaurants, changing rooms and hotels. Particular mention should be made of the long sandy beaches at Oeiras, Carcavelos, with the four star *Hotel Praia Mar*, and Parede. There are three stations with the suffix Estoril – São Pedro, São João and Monte, beyond Estoril proper. Estoril is charming, with old and new villas, dripping with bougainvillaea, begonia and climbing geranium, so

Royalty

it is not surprising that a number of exiled royalty have made their homes here and in Cascais. Ex-King Humberto of Italy, his sister the Queen Mother of Bulgaria, the Count and Countess of Barcelona and other royals come and go as they please – play golf on the well planned 18-hole course or shop in the fashionable boutiques.

Casino

Opposite the station, just above the beach, perfectly tended gardens ascend between avenues of palm trees and arcades with the tourist office, shops and restaurants, to the new casino, which opens at 15.00. Visitors can gamble (passports essential), go to the cinema, or have a luxurious dinner and watch the floor show.

The luxury hotel is the *Palacio*, haunt of VIPs and secret agents in the last war. The *Cibra*, *Lido* and *Paris* are all good hotels. The *Inglaterra* is more of a family type establishment and the *Alvorada*, near the casino has apartments with kitchens and breakfast if desired. Both the *Estalagem Belvedere* and the *Lennox* are English-run, the latter specialising in golfing holidays. There are also several pensions.

Hotels

Some of the good restaurants are located on the Avenida Biarritz and the *Frolique*, by the *Hotel Palacio*, is an amusing night club.

The Golf Club has a restaurant open to non-members. There is a nine-hole course at Linhó, on the inland road to Sintra past an autodrome with an hotel by it. Tennis players can get a game in Estoril at the club by the casino; in the wood opposite, a Country Crafts Fair is held every summer. The first resort to be developed on this coast, Monte Estoril, has excellent hotels. The *Atlantico*, on the sea, but noisy, and the *Grande* are both four star. The *Londres* and *Zenith* three star. The local restaurants serve exceptionally good food, particularly the *Bar Ingles*, expensive, with a fine view of the sea and *O Sinaleiro*, remarkably inexpensive.

Monte Estoril

Almost opposite the *Grande Hotel*, *Ray's Bar*, run by an American, is an amusing spot for a drink before or after dinner. At the bottom of the Avenida São Pedro, next to the English Bank of London and South America, *Maggie's Coffee Lounge* also serves tea and snacks and is a friendly place. On the way to Cascais, the five star *Hotel Estoril Sol* towers over the Estrada Marginal and the sea.

Cascais

Cascais has now taken over from Estoril as the smartest place on this coast in which to dine or shop. There are excellent boutiques for both men and women, good food shops and supermarkets and a very large number of restaurants at all prices. The outdoor market for local produce is on Wednesdays and Saturdays, clothing and kitchen-ware are also for sale on Wednesdays.

The *Estalagem Albatross* is installed in a private house built out on rocks just above the sea, with exceptionally good food, lovely public rooms and a few spacious bedrooms for guests. There are a couple of other hotels and several *residencias* which are adequate for room and breakfast.

At the top of the town, past the fortress which was attacked several times by the Spaniards in the 16th century, and shortly after by an English contingent sent by Queen Elizabeth I to support one of the Portuguese Pretenders to the throne, lies the Castro Guimarães park and museum.

Castro Guimarães Park and Museum

At one end of the demesne is a small zoo with monkeys, deer and a large aviary. The park is wild and wooded, with several picnic areas. The museum, in a former private house, is attractive and has good tapestries, pictures and pieces of porcelain as arranged by the owners, who left this property to the town of Cascais. There is also a public library with a section of English books.

Boca do Inferno

About half a mile along the road past the museum, lies the Boca do Inferno, or Mouth of Hell, an awesome cavity in the rocks into which the sea roars through a natural arch and makes a whirlpool, or cauldron, of spuming water. This can be a dangerous place in stormy weather and unwary visitors have been swept away. The road goes on through dunes and wild scrubland, with the occasional restaurant on the sea, and the Clube D. Carlos I, which gives temporary members an opportunity to ride, play tennis, swim in the large pool and even take a sauna bath.

Guincho Beach

Finally, the long, wide, sandy stretch of the Guincho beach, Praia do Guincho, is reached after passing two luxury hotels, the *Guincho*, in an old converted fort, and the *Muchaxo*, which specialises in sea food, and several restaurants. There is a very strong undertow on this beach and warning flags are put up when it is dangerous for swimmers. The beach is large so that even in the height of summer the sands never get uncomfortably full of people and, late in the season, the dunes above high tide are pierced with the strongly scented wild white lily, *Pancratium maritimum*.

Cabo da Roca Lighthouse

Beyond Guincho, the road turns inland through a dense wood of pine and eucalyptus. At the end, a left turn goes up through particularly lovely country to the westernmost point of the continent of Europe. The elegant lighthouse at Cabo da Roca is surrounded by the low cottages of the keepers and nearby is a pleasant café/restaurant. The main road at the top of the turning to Cabo da Roca leads on to Colares and Sintra, falling down into vine-clad country, under the western slopes of the Serra de Sintra.

Queluz and Fronteira

Queluz Palace

In the outskirts of Lisbon on the way to Sintra, Queluz is an enchanting, pink, rococo palace set on a wide, cobblestoned public square. The palace is most artfully irregular; semi-circular, one-storey wings spring out from the main block and continue off on one side to a series of pavilion-like edifices. The other side of the great open space is filled with houses contemporary with the palace, the Town Hall and Clock Tower, which make the whole a perfect ensemble of 18th century architecture.

The palace itself is one of the few Royal residences in which one could happily live. The rooms have delicately painted walls, lovely period furniture and pictures, and one apartment, the Sala das Mangas, is lined with polychrome chinoiserie tiles and chinoiserie bamboo armchairs. These are some of the loveliest secular tiles in Portugal. The gardens are formal with sphinxes in elegant ruffs looking out over the beautifully kept topiary work. Below is a

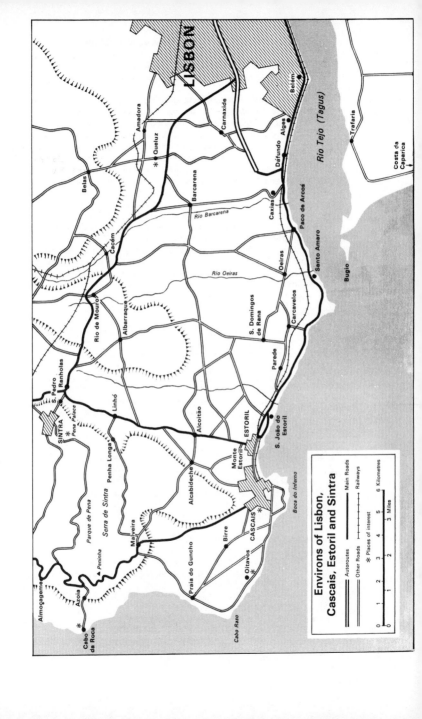

Environs of Lisbon, Cascais, Estoril and Sintra

curious Dutch canal lined with more *azulejos*, of boating scenes.

The old kitchen, of the palace is now a luxury restaurant and tea room and is a favourite venue for wedding receptions.

Fronteira
Palace
In the overgrown suburb of São Domingos de Benfica, surrounded by high-rise buildings, is the beautiful oasis of the Palace of Fronteira, with its unequalled gardens. The house is not shown to the public but the gardens can be entered by ringing at the gate and giving a tip of 20 or 50 escudos to the porter, who usually allows visitors to wander around at will. At one end of the topiary gardens a great water tank with stone steps at either side leads up to a terraced walk above, which has pyramid pavilions at either extreme roofed with copper-glazed tiles. But the great glory of this set piece lies in the 17th century tiled panels of full-sized knights on horseback in iridescent colours. Each is different and they are said to represent the *Doze de Inglaterra* who, according to legend, went to England to fight for the honour of 12 lovely English ladies. The rest of the grounds are filled with statuary, terraces and hidden nooks, and many of the walls are covered with 17th and 18th century tiled pictures of monkeys dressed up as men, driving about and forming small chattering groups.

Sintra

One of the most famous places in Portugal, Sintra, is very near to Lisbon and can be reached by road in about half an hour. There are also frequent trains from Rossio station. Sintra is noted for its remarkable vegetation and for its connection with a long line of Englishmen. Byron lived there on his visits to Portugal and a number of highly eccentric English men and women made it their home in the last century. The town has several small restaurants and the comfortable *Hotel Central* on the main square, where the tourist office is also situated.

There is a complete change in the vegetation and climate from Lisbon or Estoril and Cascais. The Serra de Sintra, a range of hills rising straight from the plain that stretches to the sea, appears to be a good deal higher than it is in reality, owing to the serrated nature of the summits and the fact that there are no foothills.

Pena Palace
The extraordinary Pena Palace with its floriated outline silhouetted against the sky, stands on one of the higher hills. This palace was built around the nucleus of an early convent by Dom Fernando, the King Consort of Queen Maria II. Begun in 1840, it is a strange conglomeration of styles from mock-Arab minarets and Gothic turrets through the Renaissance to high Victorian architecture, which can best be seen in the interior. Superbly placed, the views all around stretch from the estuary of the Tagus, the Serra da Arrábida and Setúbal to the south east, the lines of Torres Vedras to the north, Cabo da Roca to the south and the Atlantic Ocean five miles away over the plain.

38

Surrounding the palace is a wild and splendid park, with one of the best silvicultural collections in western Europe. There are groves of tree ferns, camelia trees of various colours and types, hothouses with superb gloxinias, dwarf cedars, fountains and streams, rock gardens and grottoes. The woods are a haven for birds of many varieties and hawks wheel high above. This great area is intersected by gravelled roads and cars can be taken in on payment of a small fee at the parking place below the Palace.

Pena Park

Between Pena and the Vila, or town, of Sintra lie the two other Sintra villages – São Pedro and Santa Maria; in the former there is a big country market on the second and fourth Sundays of each month, selling vegetables, fruit, kitchen-ware, amusing pottery – including plates, dishes, jugs and basins in natural red or with a yellow overglaze – clothing, junk and some antiques which are usually more expensive than in the shops. A number of stalls offer good country wine by the glass, grilled sardines and cold roast suckling pig.

São Pedro

A lane from São Pedro de Sintra, alive with fireflies in the dusk of May and June, leads under the hill to Santa Maria de Sintra, an enchanting village, around a Gothic church, one of the few very early churches near Lisbon.

Santa Maria

Between Pena and Sintra proper, is a Moorish castle dating back to the 7th century. Captured from the Moors by Afonso Henriques in 1147, the fortress gradually fell into ruin and is now a wild, strange, lonely place, with unexpectedly lovely views from the ramparts.

Castelo dos Mouros

The Palácio de Vila, or town palace is, like all great Portuguese houses and palaces, situated right on the roadway – in this case a charming square with the pretty pink-washed Misericordia Hospital below.

Town Palace

High, wide steps lead up to the palace, which is a conglomeration of architecture from Moorish to Edwardian times, having always been a Royal residence. Unlike Pena, this palace has some beautifully furnished apartments, with interesting pictures. The first part of the palace to be shown is the huge kitchen with great oasthouse chimneys to carry away the smoke and fumes from the fires for roasting, placed in the centre of the room.

The visitor is then taken through a series of apartments, all containing tiles from the very rare 15th century raised black ones in the Mermaids Room, to the fine panels in blue and white of hunting scenes in the Sala dos Brazões, where the ceiling is composed of painted panels with the arms of 72 of the noble families of Portugal. The Sala das Pegas, is so called because the ceiling is painted with a great number of magpies, each different, and each holding in its claw the Red Rose of Lancaster and, above its beak, the words *Por Bem*, as the legend says that King John I, on being caught kissing one of his English Queen's Ladies, said these words,

39

meaning 'well meant', and so had this room painted in this punning way. Perhaps the most beautiful of all the apartments is the Swan Room, with unusual green and off-white early tiles in a diamond pattern on the walls. The full-size swans, painted on the great ceiling, are each in a different position, while on the tables are superb Chinese porcelain dishes in the forms of birds, fishes and animals.

The Edwardian part of the palace, reconstructed at the beginning of this century, lies to the right of the entrance hall. There are late-Victorian portraits of the Royal Family and the furnishings are those of the early 1900s.

Seteais Palace   Just on the edge of the town, towards Seteais, is the house where Byron stayed in 1810, which is now a guest house and restaurant called the *Estalagem dos Cavaleiros*. Further along, is the exquisite Seteais Palace, built by a Dutchman at the end of the 18th century. A triumphal arch links the long low wings and this beautiful building is now a luxury hotel, superbly furnished. The main drawing room is frescoed by Pillement with forest trees, the branches and foliage meeting overhead.

About three miles beyond Seteais, lie the famous gardens of
Monserrate   Monserrate, open every day from 09.00 to 18.00. There is no entrance charge and no closing day. The gardens surrounding the extraordinary three-domed Moorish Palace that Sir Francis Cook, a rich merchant from the City of London built in 1864, were laid out by Scottish gardeners in the middle of the last century. They contain the greatest variety of ferns in the world, in addition to giant daturas, strawberry trees, Chinese gingkos, camelias, rhododendrons and an immense variety of rare trees and shrubs.

Towards the end of the road that runs from just below the Pena
Cork Convent   park along the top of the Serra de Sintra, is the Capuchos, or Cork Convent. Founded in 1560, this place is so strange that lovers of the unusual would find it well worth a visit. There are 12 tiny cells for the Franciscans who lived there, each cut out of the living rock, some still lined with cork to keep out the ever-present damp and others with cork cupboards and cork fittings. This remote place is set in a peaceful dell with marvellous wild flowers in the spring and early summer and a trickle of water tinkles into a stone basin outside the entrance.

Janus   In the small village of Janus, in the plain between Sintra and Praia das Maças, there is an extremely old circular church which must once have been a Mosque. This is set in a field and on August 17th, each year, there is a big fair and *romaria*, when people bring along their oxen, goats, sheep, pigs and dogs as São Mamede, to whom the church is dedicated, was a farmer, and this is his Feast Day.

Mafra   The immense palace of Mafra, 12 miles north of Sintra, and easily reached by bus or car from both Lisbon and Sintra, is set on a plain,

40

so that the huge edifice with two high belfries looking curiously oriental – 'the enchanted palace of a giant' – as Byron wrote, can be seen from miles away. The monastery and palace were started by King John V in 1717, in thanksgiving for the birth of a child to his wife Maria Anna of Austria. Unlike the Escorial in Spain, with which it has often been compared, Mafra, designed by John Frederic Ludwig of Ratisbon, is a cheerful place. The cunningly designed façade, pale honey in colour, over 800 feet in length, stretches out on either side of an Italianate basilica with enormous Baroque statues adorning the atrium, their marble hair and clothes billowing in the wind. At either end are flat, onion-shaped cupolas balancing the minaret-like belfries of the church, each containing carillons which are still sometimes played on Sunday afternoons in the summer months, the sound, like a giant musical box, tinkling across the surrounding countryside.

The interior, with a religious art museum which is not of great interest, contains an endless range of rooms along the front and east sides of the palace. These former Royal apartments have painted walls and ceilings and fine Empire and early-Victorian furniture. At last the Library is reached.

In Mafra Library, together with that in the University of Coimbra, Portugal possesses what are surely two of the most beautiful libraries in the world. The room here is 200 feet long and very narrow and the decoration is in off-white grisaille, giving a wonderfully serene feel to the whole beautifully proportioned space. The bookcases and the gallery above them reach up to the white plaster barrel ceiling and in each of the many windows on either side, are set contemporary tables and chairs for students. *Mafra Library*

Behind the palace, which is in the centre of the village, lies a huge park, entirely surrounded by a wall. In it roam deer, wild boar, lynx, civet cats and all manner of wild life. The chase is intersected by unmetalled roads and can be entered by visitors on foot, or in cars, by an entry along a turning off the Ericeira road to the west, which is signposted 'Gradil'. After some miles along this road, the wall is broken by an iron gate which can be overlooked from a fast car. Visitors should ring the bell when a caretaker will open the gates, usually asking to see some form of identification such as a passport and temporary address, before letting the car inside. A few hundred yards along to the left is the Hunting Museum, Museu de Caça, which consists of a large gallery with a number of stuffed animals. *Mafra Chase*

Hunting Museum

In the adjoining coach house are rows of enchanting late-Victorian and Edwardian country carriages, including dogcarts, pony traps and Victorias. One dogcart is made entirely of wickerwork and belonged to Dona Amelia, the last Queen of Portugal. The harnesses are kept on special stands and in cases round the walls and everything is in perfect condition. *Coach House*

41

Ericeira   Seven miles to the west of Mafra, on the sea, is the fishing and
beach resort of Ericeira. The town is filled with pretty whitewashed
houses though many new buildings and a large *Hotel de Turismo*
have been built on the outskirts. To the north are miles of almost
deserted beaches up to Peniche.

Setúbal Peninsula

Between the river Tagus and the river Sado to the south, lies the
Setúbal peninsula. A fast motorway (toll 30 escudos), leads from
the Tagus bridge (toll 20 escudos), to the large industrial town of
Setúbal on the river Sado, 30 miles away. This peninsula has lovely
country, splendid buildings, good beaches to the south and long
sandy beaches on the Atlantic, many without road approaches.

Setúbal   Busy and prosperous, Setúbal is one of the most ancient cities in
Portugal and was known to have existed before the time of the first
king. The main industries are fishing, sardine canning and now,
shipbuilding at the big shipyards of Setenave, built out on a sandy
spit a little way up the river. A wide avenue is bordered by the
docks and the ferry station for boats taking cars across to the
Peninsula of Troia, now being developed as a tourist centre, and
the start of one of the best roads down to the western part of the
Algarve.

Jesus Church   Setúbal contains one of the most famous churches in Portugal,
that of Jesus, started in 1494, its twisting pillars of many coloured
Arrábida marble showing the birth pangs of the Manueline style.
For this building presages all the fantasies which came a little later
in the Jeronimos church in Belem, the Abbey of Batalha and the
many other Manueline buildings in the country. The church closes
at 17.00.

Museum   At the side of the church, the museum is housed in the former
conventual buildings. The collection includes a unique set of six
large grisaille canvases of the Passion of Christ. They are painted in
the Chinese style with 18th century Chinese figures and set in false
frames of painted red velvet. There is also the great set of religious
pictures by the Master of Setúbal, a Portuguese primitive painter,
which at one time hung high on the walls of the Jesus church.

Bomfim   Lovers of the wildest Baroque should see the chapel of Senhor do
Chapel   Bomfim at the end of the park of the same name. It is small, lined
with vivid blue tiled panels of religious scenes and canvases
above, set in superb gilded woodwork which also fills the chancel
and side altars. The painted coffered ceiling depicts flowers and
classical motifs, with strangely shaped dogs and men amidst
arabesques. The chapel is open from 15.00 to 18.00 every afternoon, except on Saturdays. Another gold-filled chapel is that of
Corpo Santo near the great parish church of Santa Maria da Graça.
But almost every church in the town is of interest, and in the
eastern part of the city there is a fine early 18th century archway.

42

Setúbal is also famous for wine and good food. Azeitão cheese is from this area. The *Clube Naval*, on the main avenue has excellent fish, including red mullet (salmonete) baked in the oven with olive oil and breadcrumbs; and the *Bocage*, in the Praça of the same name, serves delicious Portuguese food, such as veal cutlets stewed in a casserole with sliced onions and potatoes. All the small restaurants by the docks also have hearty fish and meat dishes with the local wine. Muscatel brandy and the sweet, fortified Muscatel and Setúbal wines, all taste of Muscatel grapes and are produced in the region. The luxury *Pousada de São Filipe* (tel. (065) 23844/24981), is in an old fortress just outside the town.

Restaurants

Accommoda-tion

Up the river, the pyramids of salt left to dry in the sun are an interesting feature of the landscape, and further up the valley, rice is grown extensively.

The most beautiful way to approach Setúbal is through the peninsula, turning right for Sesimbra at the end of the first part of the motorway from the Lisbon bridge. This road winds through groves of umbrella pines and woods of eucalyptus to Sesimbra, a fishing village on the open sea. Unlike most of the seaside resorts in Portugal, unbridled development of apartment houses has taken place on the outskirts. The actual village and the fishermen's beach still have charm, and in the Misericordia Hospital, now an old people's home, is a famous picture of Our Lady of Mercy. On a hill behind the town, stands the much restored castle with a little archaeological museum adjoining. There are numerous restaurants and two hotels – the four star *Mar* and two star *Espadarte* on the sea.

Sesimbra

Below Sesimbra castle the main road carries on due west to Cape Espichel, with a lighthouse, and nearby the beautiful pilgrimage centre of Nossa Senhora do Cabo. Go under the archway at the side of the church on to the windswept turf, bright with wild flowers, above the high cliffs. At the edge is a domed chapel with *azulejos* panels seen through the grilled door. Have your picnic in the shade on the north side of the church with the Sintra hills visible in the far distance, on clear days, and a superb sweep of untouched sandy beaches reaching up to Caparica. No roads lead to these unsullied sands, which take the full force of the Atlantic rollers. The church is usually shut but there is a big *romaria* on August 15th when all the local people gather for the festivities, as they do on the last Sunday of September when the fishermen come on pilgrimage.

Cape Espichel

The same road back, past the turning to Sesimbra, takes the traveller to the Serra da Arrábida, a range of hills which, to the south, rises almost directly from the estuary of the Sado, and to the north from cultivated lands, finally reaching the Tagus. The limestone ridge, in places over 2,000 ft in height, is still covered in places with the untouched original forest of the peninsula. The great variety of wild flowers includes a peony, tulips, ophrys, the Iberian

Serra da Arrábida

bluebell and a snowdrop found only in this place. Badgers and other wild creatures, breed and nest on these rocky slopes.

Portinho da Arrábida

Before the range is reached, a turning to the right winds round the side of the mountains until a right fork leads to Portinho da Arrábida where a long sickle-shaped beach with unusually large grained sand, borders the sea, which is so blue and so translucent that swimmers can see right down to the sea bed, many feet below them. There are many small restaurants but in the summer months parking is extremely difficult. A little way up the hill from Portinho a road to Setúbal is cut into the side of the hills just above the sea. Further up, a spectacular road goes to Setúbal over the summit of the range. From here, it is almost as though the views of the estuary of the Sado and the long promontory of Troia far below, are seen from an aeroplane.

Palmela

To the north of Setúbal lies the huge Templars' castle of Palmela, on a high escarpment of hill at the east end of the Serra da Arrábida. Much of the medieval system of this splendid ruin can still be traced. The views on either side, to Lisbon on the north and to Setúbal on the south, are stunning and on fine days the harmonious moaning of the clay whistles on the sails of the windmills just below the castle, rises into the clear air. A superb luxury *pousada*

Accommoda-tion

(tel. 2351226/2351395), has been installed in the beautifully restored and converted 18th century section of the castle, a perfect place for the visitor to stay or just lunch or dine. A pool is another of its amenities. The slopes of the town below the castle are filled with narrow streets and alleyways through 17th and 18th century houses, many of them built of stone from the castle which was largely destroyed by the earthquake of 1755.

The old road from Setúbal to Cacilhas, where there is a ferry (taking cars) over the Tagus to Lisbon, passes one of the earliest inhabited houses in Portugal, that of Bacalhoa, which was bought in 1528 by the son of Afonso de Albuquerque, the first Viceroy of Portuguese India. The house, which is not open to the public, is crowned by cantaloupe melon-like cupolas at each corner of the T-shaped building. The gardens, usually shown on request, are formal with low hedges of clipped box surrounding orange and lemon trees and, at the end, a great basin is backed by a low, elegant pavilion with three pyramided towers. In this pavilion is the earliest dated tiled panel in Portugal, that of Susannah and the Elders, 1565.

Quinta das Torres

A short way beyond, near Vila Fresca de Azeitão, the *Quinta das Torres*, a beautiful private house, is now an admirably run guest house with a good restaurant. The house is washed by a large water tank from the centre of which rises a small classical pavilion. On the other side is the courtyard, with stabling and coach houses and all the offices around which a large estate used to revolve. In the woods near the house there is a natural pool which guests use for swimming. An ideal centre for seeing this lovely part of the country, so near to Lisbon and yet seeming very remote.

44

Beach at Albufeira

Algarve

The great majority of visitors to Portugal fly straight to Faro in the Algarve, the southernmost province, and spend most of their time on the superb beaches, warm and sunny for the greater part of the year, and sample delicious seafood in the many restaurants. The fish is caught locally and often sold by the fishermen on the beach when their boats come in. Bream (pargo), smelts (carapau), sardines, grey mullet (tainha), skate (raia), whiting (pescada), squids (lulas) and fresh tunny are cooked in casseroles with onions and coriander or bay leaves, baked with olive oil and lemon or plain boiled with turnip tops.

Those who like to vary their sunbathing with sightseeing are often led to believe that there is nothing of interest in the Algarve. However, this is far from true.

The very province is mysterious. The name comes from the Arabic *el gharb*, and it was the last part of Portugal to be occupied by the Muslims, who were only finally expelled in 1250, a hundred years after Lisbon was freed by British crusaders fighting alongside the Portuguese. Many of the place names are of unmistakable Arabic origin and so remote was it from the rest of Portugal that, through the centuries, the monarchs were Kings of Portugal *and* the Algarve.

There is much Moorish feeling in the architecture and the people themselves are different, more reserved than those from other parts of the country. Even the way they speak Portuguese is often difficult to understand.

History

Before the Algarve was invaded by the Moors in 711, this southern coast had been settled by the Phoenicians and Carthaginians, and the Greeks are known to have been here. But it was the Romans who left their mark with countless remains including the large buildings at Milreu. When they left in the 5th century, the Visigoths came in and were turned out by the Moors.

*Prince Henry
the Navigator*

The most famous man in the history of the Algarve is Prince Henry the Navigator, son of King John I and his English Queen Philippa of Lancaster, daughter of John of Gaunt. Henry made his headquarters at Sagres, the extreme western promontory of the region, and evidence remains that it was here that the Prince gathered all that was surmised about the then unknown world beyond Cape Bojador in Africa.

He collated all the facts that he learnt, designed the ships that bore his captains into the unknown and, as a result of his research and planning in this remote corner of Europe, Portugal discovered and explored over half the inhabited globe in the course of the 15th and 16th centuries.

Faro, three miles from the international airport, is on the coast in the centre of the hundred mile stretch of country which forms the Algarve. Only 40 miles in depth, the Algarve is separated from the Alentejo by low mountainous ranges from which the country falls down to long sandy beaches. The land is covered in almond blossom at the end of January and beginning of February, and later the low broody masses of fig trees break into leaf, interspersed with oranges and lemons grown in regular lines. Strawberries and tomatoes are ripened early in plastic hothouses.

There is a single track railway line crossing the length of the Algarve from Vila Real de Sto Antonio in the east to Lagos in the west, via Tunes, the junction for Lisbon. This train meanders along through fascinating country, stopping at tiny stations which are elegantly adorned with glazed pictorial tiles.

Faro

A prosperous, busy city with a yacht basin in the centre. The hotels *Eva* (four star) and *Faro* (three star) overlook the ever changing scene, the former with a rooftop pool and excellent views. Close to the yacht basin and a public garden is the tourist office and the lovely Arco da Vila, a Renaissance archway leading to the medieval part of the town, surrounded by thick walls in which are three other archways.

46

The Largo da Sé, or Cathedral Square, is a delightful uneven space surrounded by the whitewashed cathedral, the bishop's palace and low, elegant buildings with curious roofs shaped like a series of pyramids, the tiles softened by age into delicate pinks and yellows. The bones of the cathedral are Gothic with later additions – a red Chinoiserie organ, a pair of Nubians holding lamps, a wildly Baroque altar to the right with a statue of Our Lady and the Holy Child under a miniature baldachino supported on the heads of angels, and a curious relic chapel in grisaille. Pillaged by the Earl of Essex, the bishop's library formed the nucleus of the Bodleian in Oxford. *Cathedral*

After all this richness, the simple museum in the restored Convent of Nossa Senhora da Assuncão, behind the cathedral, is a great contrast. There are archaeological remains from Roman and pre-Roman eras, some agreeable religious paintings, a small section devoted to military memorabilia and an enormous early 19th century chair, said to be that of the bishop, which for some reason must have been removed from the cathedral. A pretty double cloister completes the ensemble. *Museums*

There is also a Maritime Museum on the sea at the side of the *Hotel Eva*. Entrance is free but it is closed on Saturday afternoons and Sunday. The exhibits are upstairs, alongside the city library, showing ship models, fishing nets, accurate paintings of local fish and models of navigational aids. The other museums in Faro are the Regional Ethnological in the District Board building, the Ferreira de Almeida Art Collection in the Town Hall and the Museu Antonino by the Belvedere of Santo Antonio do Alto.

As has been stressed, the most notable architecture in Portugal is ecclesiastical, and apart from the cathedral, there are several very fine churches in Faro with splendid Baroque features and interesting canvases. São Francisco in the huge Largo de S. Francisco is a fantastic jewel within a plain exterior. Open from 07.30 to 11.30 and 16.30 to 19.00, the unique feature of this single-aisled church is the central octagon, rising to a dome at the entrance to the chancel. The walls are entirely covered with the finest quality Baroque gold work. There are altars at each corner with noble polychrome carved statues of saints and under the dome four elegant balconies with no purpose except to complete the wild fantasy of the whole conception. Blue and white glazed tiles of the life of St Francis add to the riot of colour and there are even pictorial tiles in the roof of the chancel. *São Francisco*

Other fine churches in Faro are those of São Pedro in the Largo de São Pedro, which is also filled with untouched gold Baroque woodwork, beautiful statues and *azulejos* of St Peter in a Rococo chapel to the right; the elegant ambones are approached by curving stairs. Behind São Pedro, in the Largo do Carmo, the huge Baroque façaded Carmo church is only open from 11.00 to midday and from 15.00 to 16.00. This also has Baroque features within, *São Pedro*

Carmo

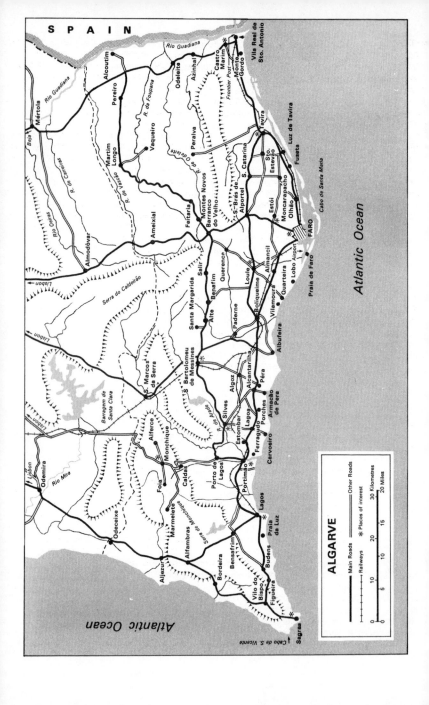

some good Portuguese primitives and a lively statue of Our Lady of Mount Carmel by the 18th century sculptor, Machado de Castro. A big regional fair is held in front of this church in the last two weeks of July and one of the most important fairs in the Algarve, that of Santa Iria, takes place from October 19th to 27th each autumn. You can buy not only agricultural implements, cattle, horses, mules, donkeys and pigs in these fairs, but also rough pottery utensils, tinware, wooden bowls and spoons, as well as country produce.

Faro beach is long and sandy and is actually situated on an island just off the town. It can be reached by road or by a regular ferry service which gives a marvellous view of the white houses and belfries of Faro rising from the sea. The beach is well appointed with changing rooms, restaurants, bars, the *Estalagem Aeromar* (four star) and many amenities. *Beach*

The country to the west of Faro, the Barlavento, is more attractive than the Sotavento to the east, so we shall now go along this coast with its splendid beaches, to Sagres and Cape St Vincent, with a brief look at some of the inland places of major interest. The main road which goes the whole length of the Algarve, is not a motorway and is some way inland, so secondary roads go down to the little villages on the water's edge, many of which have been turned into tourist complexes. *Barlavento*

Ten miles from Faro Airport, Vale do Lobo is one of the biggest developments in the region, covering some 750 acres with an 18-hole golf course, designed by Henry Cotton, swimming pools, tennis and squash courts. There are apartments and villas to rent. The five star *Hotel D. Filipa* is almost on the beach. *Vale do Lobo*

Adjoining Vale do Lobo, the Quinta do Lago has apartments by a natural sea-water lagoon, 27-hole golf course and a riding centre. *Quinta do Lago*

The entire interior of the church of São Lourenço outside Almansil is lined with vivid blue and white glazed 18th century tiles, the walls with scenes from the life of the early Christian martyr, the domed ceiling with formal architectural conceits. The high altar is of high quality Baroque gold work soaring up to meet the *azulejos* in the roof. Adjoining is a new Art Centre run by an English couple. *São Lourenço*

Inland, Loulé is a busy town in the centre of rich agricultural country. The castle occupies a large space in the very centre of the town and, unlike most castles, is not on a hill. The Gothic parish church is set in an exceptionally pretty square, the interior has three aisles and is wide and light, with a Manueline arch leading to the chancel, good gold work and fine *azulejo* panels. *Loulé*

Outside the town is the small pilgrimage chapel of Nossa Senhora da Piedade; at the *romaria* held on April 15th or the nearest Sunday to that date, the statue of Our Lady is carried out in procession through the town. Note the pair of painted angels in Renaissance military costumes which stand within this small shrine.

From Loulé a road north-east through Querença joins one of the routes north from the Algarve to Lisbon, winding through the Malhão range of low hills to Almodovar and Aljustrel in the Alentejo.

Quarteira Quarteira is one of the oldest fishing villages in the Algarve and has a very long, sandy beach. There are apartments and villas, the four star *Hotel Quarteira-Sol* and the *Beira Mar* and *D. José*, both three-star, as well as several pensions. Good restaurants include *O Barão*, three km away on the Loulé road, with excellent food cooked by the Russian wife of the English owner. It is open for dinners only and shut on Mondays.

Vilamoura A complete tourist centre, Vilamoura has apartments, holiday villages, motels and hotels, and a long sandy beach. The two 18-hole golf courses were designed by Frank Pennink; other facilities are a riding centre, swimming pools, marina, gambling casino, shopping centres and airstrip.

Falésia Near the Acoteias beach, with gently rolling pine-covered land falling down to a sweeping sandy beach, with high cliffs on either side, Falésia is a development with accommodation for a thousand people in villas of every size. Ample social facilities include restaurants, bars, swimming pools, tennis, riding, night club and an outdoor theatre. Also the four star Hotel *Alfa Mar*.

Beaches The beaches of Olhos de Agua, Maria Luisa, Balaia and Oura lie between Falésia and Albufeira, are easy to get down to from the higher land behind them, and are blessedly free from over-development.

Albufeira The attractive town of Albufeira is the most popular place in the Algarve, yet has managed to preserve much of the charm of a typical Portuguese village. Small whitewashed houses, long and low, some with coats of arms above the doorways, line the narrow streets, often passing under Moorish arches. The main beach is reached by a short tunnel cutting through the rock and the fishermen's beach to the east is down a ramp. The tourist office is in the Rua 5 de Outubro.

Albufeira was once an important fortress and only fell to King Afonso III in 1250, being one of the last towns in the Algarve to be held by the Moors. The fish market, open every morning, displays the great variety of fish from these waters and buyers will experience the very different taste of seafood when it is *really* fresh and not frozen before being eaten. There is also a big market on Saturday mornings when the country people come in to sell their produce, so you can buy succulent blue or green figs in their season, the fruits of the arbutus tree, looking like small scarlet sea urchins, which make an excellent liqueur; peaches and nectarines and, in the early part of the year, large sweet oranges which can be seen growing all over the Algarve, to say nothing of freshly picked almonds and walnuts.

The *Hotel da Balaia* (five star) is five km east of Albufeira, a notably comfortable hotel with its own sandy beach, swimming pool, tennis, sailing, water skiing and a night club. In or near the town are the *Sol e Mar*, on the beach and the *Montechoro* a little further away (both four star). There are several two and three star hotels, apartments and a large number of pensions. The night life is smart and crowded and there are numberless restaurants and bars, including Sir Harry's Bar just off the main square, under English management.

Hotels

North of Albufeira, São Bartolomeu de Messines, with bright whitewashed houses, has a very unusual parish church; short, twisted stone columns in the local veined marble of reddish tones, separate the three aisles. These twisted columns, which appear in very few churches in Portugal, are the first manifestation of what was soon to become the Manueline style.

São Bartolomeu de Messines

Off the road due-east from São Bartolomeu de Messines to the pretty village of Alte, there is another of the main routes to Lisbon, via São Marcos da Serra in the Algarve, and Ourique and Castro Verde, in the Alentejo. Around an hour's walk from Alte there is an enormous cave, the Buraco dos Mouros, with three huge chambers leading into one another.

Alte

Buraco dos Mouros

Back on the coast west of Albufeira are the pleasant beaches of Baleeira, São Rafael, Castelo and Galé, all easy of access. Some have only tracks leading down to them, and have not yet been much developed. The onetime pleasant village of Armação da Pera, is now in the centre of highrise apartment houses and straggling streets. However, Armação is redeemed by having one of the longest beaches in the Algarve, from which fishermen still set forth in their boats each night and bring back the catch to be auctioned off on the beach. Some of the red sandstone rock formations on the shore form sheltered enclaves and to the west beyond the Praia Senhora da Rocha, with the five star *Hotel Viking*, the sea has hollowed out a curious series of caverns and grottoes to which an excursion by boat is easily arranged through the local tourist office. The *Hotel Garbe*, the *Hotel do Levante*, The *Albergaria Cimar* and the *Estalagem Algar* are all four star.

Beaches

Armação da Pera

Another delightful, rather remote beach near Senhora da Rocha is Praia das Gaivotas. Like the beaches nearby, Alfranzinha and Algar Seco, it is situated below cliffs.

Beaches

The beach of Carvoeiro is sheltered, but surrounded by new developments including the large Quinta do Paraiso with villas, restaurants and sporting facilities.

Estombar	Estombar, on the main road from Faro, a few miles before reaching Portimão, is a beautiful, white Algarvian town, covering a low hill to the right of the main road and crowned with a huge church; the great Baroque façade, topped by two onion-shaped belfries, rather anachronistically surrounds a very fine Manueline door. Inside the church 18th century *azulejos* border the windows and the arches of the aisles. The chandeliers are notable, as they are so often in village churches in Portugal.
Silves	A few miles to the north, Silves, once the seat of a bishopric, was the Moorish capital, then known as Chelb, and a busy port on the river Arade. Now the river is so silted up that no ships of any size can come up from the sea at Portimão. Although Silves is one of the earliest cities in the Algarve, there is not much of interest apart from a noble castle and the cathedral. It was besieged for six weeks in 1189 when the combined fleets of the Portuguese and the English Crusaders sailed down from Lisbon to Portimão, and went on up the river Arade to attack the city, which capitulated six weeks later. Lagos, Portimão and Monchique surrendered soon after, but Faro and the Sotavento were only wrested from the Moors 60 years later under King Afonso III.
Castle	The castle has huge water cisterns below, built by the Moors to withstand the endless sieges of that period. These still supply water to the town. The great building covers a large area, and is one of the most remarkable military fortifications left by the Arabs in Portugal.
Cathedral	The Gothic cathedral is not large. There are several early tombs believed to be those of the Crusaders who helped to capture the town, and in one of the side chapels an unusual architrave of carved wood imitating the adjacent Gothic arch.
	A Roman bridge crosses the river Arade and a country market is held on the quays. The finely carved Cross of Portugal now stands just outside the town; on one side is the Crucifixion and on the other, the Descent from the Cross.
Ferragudo	Overlooking the broad estuary of the river Arade, this small town, crowned by a ruined castle rises high opposite Portimão. There is a good sandy beach which is easy of access and a number of restaurants and night-spots.
Portimão	Another delightful Algarve city, Portimão is one of the busiest after Faro. A long road bridge crosses the wide river as does the railway bridge a little further up. The town is one of the best shopping centres in the Algarve. In Rua Santa Isabel you can buy not only good modern pictures and sculpture in the Galerias Portimão, but also Charles Jourdain shoes much cheaper than in Britain, and fine porcelain and pottery in several of the elegant little shops, mostly run by their owners. There are no buildings of particular note in Portimão, but the whole place is curiously attractive as it is a

52

deep-water port where dozens of fishing boats unload their catches. By the bridge and on the quayside are several simple restaurants with excellent grilled fresh fish and local wine served in jugs. The *Hotel Globo* is three star as is the *Residencial San Carlo*.

From Portimão a road goes north to Monchique. Set on the upper slopes of the Serra de Monchique, one of the ranges of hills which separates the Algarve from the rest of Portugal, the scenery is verdant and wooded, not unlike that of Sintra; the little town itself is prosperous and pleasant and is considerably cooler in the summer than the coast some 12 miles away. Just above the town is the ruined convent of Nossa Senhora do Desterro which cannot be reached by car; for energetic walkers it is worth going up and climbing the tower with its fantastic view over the great plain of the Algarve. The main building is early Renaissance and much of its beauty lies in its unrestored state.

Monchique

A road from Monchique past the four star *Estalagem Abrigo da Montanha*, leads almost due west to Foia, which has one of the most famous views in the country. It is on the summit of the Serra de Monchique and is marked by an obelisk. Some say that on a very clear day, the hills of Sintra can be seen from here, but even on a normal day there is an unparalleled panorama of Lagos and Portimão and the bare country stretching to Sagres and Cape St Vincent, with a glimpse of the highly cultivated land towards Faro.

Foia

On the way up to Monchique, the Caldas, or Spa, lies just off the road to the left. It has been renovated and brought up to date as the hot spring waters are extremely good for rheumatism and intestinal disorders. There are a couple of simple pensions and the four star *Albergaria Lageado* in the somewhat melancholy but rather charming little place set within wooded slopes at the top of the valley.

Monchique Spa

Beyond Monchique there is a beautiful, extremely winding road which goes north to Lisbon passing near the *Pousada de Santa Clara*, (tel. (0083) 52250), which is in the Alentejo, beside an artificial lake.

A mile or two from Portimão and opposite Ferragudo, is Praia da Rocha, which was the first beach in the Algarve to have an hotel. There are steps down to the wide sandy beach with strange rose-coloured rocks rising from the sea. The hotels – the five star *Algarve*, four star *Jupiter* and *Tarik* and the three star *Bela Vista*, *Rocha* and the *late* apartments – are all just above the beach or very near to it. There are also a number of *estalagems* and pensions as well as restaurants and discos.

Accomodation

The three sandy beaches of Vau, Prainha, and Tres Irmãos are all slightly to the west of Portimão. Each is different and each is very easy of access. The big development of villas and apartments is well planned and overlooks the sea; many have their own seawater swimming pools.

There is a spectacular view from the five star *Hotel Alvor Praia*. The village of Alvor is a little way inland from the tourist developments with pretty old cottages grouped around the parish church, which has a very grand Manueline door ornamented with shells and animals.

Golf

The five star luxury *Hotel do Golf de Penina*, lies inland from Alvor on the main Portimão-Lagos road, past the casino, the restaurant of which has a floor show. Henry Cotton designed the 18-hole championship course as well as the two nine-hole courses. The rooms and suites face an Olympic-size swimming pool and the golf course is set in beautifully tended grounds. This hotel is planning to build a marina on one of the many inlets of the sea between Alvor and Meia Praia. Most of the unmetalled tracks on the seaward side of the main road lead to wonderful country and these deserted tidal inlets.

Odeáxere Dam

The Odeáxere dam is reached by a narrow road nine miles north from the village of Odeáxere on the road to Lagos. An irrigated valley in which melons, tomatoes, maize and all kinds of produce are grown, leads to the foothills of the Serra de Monchique in which is situated this great stretch of water.

Golf

Palmares golf course, the newest in the Algarve, was designed by Frank Pennink, five of the 18 holes being situated on the dunes, as were the original golf links at St Andrew's in Scotland. The remaining holes are sited along slightly undulating land with fine views of the sea and the bay of Lagos, and the Monchique mountains to the north.

Lagos

The large and elegant town of Lagos is situated on the great bay of the same name. Across the bridge a wide road runs alongside the bay to the Ponta de Piedade, a high rocky cape. The town contains a famous showpiece, the Baroque chapel of Santo Antonio with charming 18th century canvases of the miracles of St Anthony of Padua who was born in Lisbon, though he ended his days as a famous preacher in Italy. The very fine gold work covers the whole chapel and there is a beautiful organ loft.

Museum

The regional museum is entered at the side of the chapel and contains an extraordinary mixture of exhibits including ships models, fishing nets, shells, books, pictures and a portable altar of St Anthony, which accompanied the Portuguese army when they fought alongside the British in the Peninsular War.

At the time of the Moorish occupation, Lagos was one of the main centres of trade between Portugal and Africa. Indeed, the only slave market in Portugal was held under the arches of the Customs

House. Among numerous restaurants, the *Alpendre* off the main square is four star, with a good menu and wine list. Less expensive are *Barroca* – where caldeirada (fish stew) is a speciality – *Casa Branca* on the river and *Porta Velha*, which specialises in charcoal grills. Good hotels are the four star *Hotel de Lagos*, the three star *Hotel São Cristóvão* and *Motel de Turismo*.

Beyond the Ponta de Piedade, the Praia de Dona Ana, with the four star *Hotel Golfinho* on the cliffs above, is reached by very long stairs; the sandy beach is surrounded at low tide by rocks forming natural arches.

Beaches

The Praia de Porta de Mos, beyond Praia de Dona Ana, is surrounded by low cliffs and has a large camping ground.

From Lagos a road leads up to Alfambra, one of the main routes north to Lisbon, but most visitors will go on from Lagos to Sagres and Cape St Vincent.

A few miles outside Lagos, a turning to the left leads to the lovely Praia da Luz with one of the earliest and most attractive villa complexes in the Algarve. Both Luz Bay Club, with three swimming pools and restaurants and Luz Park have a number of well furnished private villas for renting for short or long periods. The whitewashed houses are built in the real Algarvian style and blend in exceptionally well with the old fishing village around the bay, where there are some good restaurants.

Another fine beach is the Praia do Burgau, with little development but a couple of good restaurants, the *Casa Grande* with English owners and the *Ancora*, overlooking the sea.

Salema is a singularly unspoilt village; old cottages go down to the long sandy beach where fishing boats are drawn up. There are few modern houses and the new developments are on the higher ground behind.

The beaches of Igrejinha and Martinhal, reached by side roads, are unspoilt with little development so far, though in the summer there are many campers.

Just off the main road to the right, is the unusual chapel of Nossa Senhora de Guadalupe, a 13th century Romanesque-Gothic building which is believed to be the very chapel in which Henry the Navigator prayed, for it is known that at one time he lived in the village of Raposeira nearby. There is a good Manueline door to the chapel which has been so cleaned up that it has lost much of its original charm. The columns have unusual capitals with human and animal heads as well as shells and vegetation.

Raposeira

On the road beyond Raposeira, Vila do Bispo is a cheerful, whitewashed village with an exceptionally fine church lined with

Vila do Bispo

blue and white *azulejos* in a carpet pattern, below a coffered ceiling painted with flowers and arabesques. There are also splendid chandeliers and the high altar retable and chancel arch are outlined in Baroque gold woodwork.

Sagres

The country now gets more and more arid with outcrops of stone. Aloes and low heath cover the sparse earth with the occasional patch of deep red cultivated soil, until the twin capes of Sagres and St Vincent can be seen ahead. Although now surrounded by a straggling township, the great fortress is deeply evocative to any traveller who cares for the achievements of the past, for here Prince Henry the Navigator planned the routes taken by all the first Portuguese explorers out into the Atlantic and down the west coast of Africa, until 60 years after the Navigator's death Vasco da Gama rounded the Cape of Good Hope and opened the sea route to the Indies and the Orient.

Fortress

The ever-open fortress with a tunnel-like entrance through which cars can be driven into the huge space, is lonely and bare. To the left a curious stone compass dial pushes up from the sparsely covered ground. This was only discovered in 1928 and is possibly contemporary with the Navigator. There are still lengths of the original walls though many were rebuilt after the great earthquake of 1755 which destroyed much of the original masonry. A youth hostel occupies a long, low building by the tourist office. The small chapel of Our Lady of Grace is, unfortunately, usually shut because of the danger of vandalism. A short film on the life and achievements of Prince Henry, in English, French, German and Portuguese is shown at different times throughout the day; the tourist office will give the times.

Baleeira

A cove with a sandy beach lies just below the point, with the beautifully located three star *Hotel de Baleeira*. There is a seawater pool, for the beaches of this southernmost point of Europe receive the full force of the Atlantic, and are therefore unsafe for any but the strongest swimmers.

The luxury *Pousada do Infante* (tel. (0082) 64222/3) is just above the Praia da Mareta where there are a couple of good restaurants with excellent fresh fish.

Belixe

Between the two capes a luxury restaurant has been installed in the Belixe fort, with a tourist menu as well as à la carte. There is some accommodation. From the battlements visitors can look down at the restless waters far below, reached by a catwalk over the rocks for fishermen or the very sure-footed.

Cape
St Vincent

Cape St Vincent, to the north of Sagres, is famous for the battle in which Nelson and Jarvis defeated the French in 1797 and immortalised in Robert Browning's poem, 'Nobly, nobly, Cape St Vincent, To the North-west died away'; the huge lighthouse has an exceptionally bright light and the reflectors are said to be the strongest in

Europe, throwing a beam 60 miles out to sea. Visitors are welcome to go over the installation and up to the lighthouse, reached through a gate in the fortress walls which, unlike those at Sagres, surround only the tip of the Cape. It is often very rough and extremely windy even in the summer. Looking out, the sea below is an astonishingly deep blue.

North of Vila do Bispo a road leads up to Bordeira and ultimately on to Lisbon. Side roads go off to the left to completely unspoiled and lonely beaches. The first of these is Castalejo, a few miles to the north of the Torre de Aspa, the tallest rock in the Algarve. This tiny beach is one of the few in the Algarve with no sand except at low tide. The road goes down a narrow valley with high cliffs on either side and not a house has been built as yet in this lonely place, ideal for bird watchers. The countryside all around is singularly beautiful and for some miles the main road winds through groves of umbrella pines, while pyramid-shaped hills rise suddenly from the pastures on either side.

Castalejo Beach

The large village of Aljezur, orginally founded by the Arabs, lies along a narrow river. The castle, which can only be reached on foot, crowns a low hill. Over the river is the new town founded by the local Bishop in 1795, owing to the belief that the old town by the river was unhealthily low-lying.

Aljezur

Two roads out of Aljezur lead to the beaches of Arrifana and Monte Clerigos; the former is reached by a very steep cobbled road with hairpin bends down the cliff. There are very few houses and perfect peace. A tall rock rears up from the sea, a hundred yards from the beach.

Arrifana

On the road, halfway between Aljezur and the coast is the *Vale de Telha*, a large new tourist project in which it is planned to have hotels, restaurants, a golf course, tennis and every kind of amenity. Also on the coast, easily reached from Vale de Telha, are the sandy beaches of Pipa and Amoreira, with as yet few buildings.

The very wide and sandy Monte Clerigos beach lies across the silted-up estuary of a river crossed by a primitive bridge. Monte Clerigos is approached by a particularly lovely road going slightly north-west of Aljezur, with views of the octagonal walls of the castle and its two towers and the 18th century town in the distance.

Monte Clerigos

Odeceixe lies up a steep hill just off the road north, and is the last village in the Algarve before Odemira in the southern Alentejo. As its purely Arabic name suggests, the whole place looks strangely Moorish. Skirting the village is another lovely road leading along a wide valley with a stream in the middle, to the beach of Odeceixe. A few houses, all letting rooms in the summer, and some cafés and restaurants face the long sandy space, perfect for camping or a really remote and peaceful holiday.

Odeceixe

East of Faro

Sotavento

To the east of Faro there are long islets protecting the flat coast. These afford splendid sheltered bathing and good sailing. Inland are various fascinating places including a notable country house behind Faro.

Estoi
Palace

The small village of Estoi, about six miles north of Faro, lies off the main road to Lisbon and contains a famous 18th century house, now an elegant Sleeping Beauty of a palace. Stone steps lead down from the artfully irregular pink façade to a pool, where there are groups of statuary and a winter garden; on an upper terrace is a glass-fronted room containing a strange Christmas crib made of cork, with a hundred or more figures of Algarvian country people grouped around the Mother and Child. There are also a pair of gazebos and a marvellous view over the countryside to the sea in the distance. Strangely enough, the tiles of this 18th century summer pleasance are all pure *art nouveau*. Huge magnolia trees, with old-fashioned roses climbing up them, adorn the lower gardens.

The grounds are open to the public. For admission, ring the heavy bell at the iron gates leading to a palm tree avenue with stables and cow byres on one side. One of the caretakers will take visitors up to the deserted terraces and should be tipped 50 escudos, as there is no entrance fee and he may come from quite a distance in the large demesne. Many of the specimens in the garden are of great rarity, including a mountain immortelle from the Andes which is cultivated there to give shade to young coffee plants. In the spring the bright red flowers completely cover the branches before a leaf appears, as do the flowers of Judas trees and, in most years, the jacarandas burst into blue flower before their leaves appear.

Estoi palace is the only country house of any importance in the whole of the Algarve, showing how remote the province has always been from the rest of the country. There are few conventual remains except in the towns, where fine old family houses and monasteries still stand.

Milreu

Half a mile to the west of Estoi are the Roman remains of Milreu, just to the north of the road. There is a ruined apse standing in a field and quantities of broken columns, mosaics and stone inscriptions; little real excavation has been done over the years, though most of the museums in the Algarve contain exhibits from this site.

São Bráz de
Alportel

On the road north to Lisbon, this village on a cross-roads has one of the excellent state pousadas, *Pousada de São Bráz* (tel. (0089) 42305), with a fantastic view down to Faro.

Olhão

The greatest fishing port in the Algarve, Olhão was founded in the 16th century. It is the centre for tunny fishing and the pair of large Edwardian brick-red market buildings stand out incongruously by the beach, but they are the best markets in the Algarve. One is devoted to fish of every conceivable kind landed from the fishing fleets which go out every night, the other sells fruit, vegetables and meat. There are excellent shops with goods of every sort, at lower prices than in the tourist centres, and the town has an air of bustling prosperity. To see the much-vaunted cubist nature of the low square houses, you must climb a church tower or some other building, then look down on the roofs each surrounded by a low wall and with a staircase leading up to it from inside the house. It is believed in the Algarve that the women of this town are more beautiful than in any other part of the province.

A side road inland from Olhão leads to the pretty village of Moncarapacho, with a museum alongside the Santo Cristo chapel. *Moncarapacho* Neolithic and Roman remains from Milreu are on show, and a very good selection of church ornaments and vessels, as well as a most unusual Italian nativity scene with dozens of figures. The chapel is lined with carpet *azulejos* and fine early painted panels on the high altar retable. There are also four unusual early-Gothic metal crosses. The two other churches in this large village are both of interest. The parish church, fundamentally Gothic, has a Renaissance doorway, more carpet *azulejos*, and another unusual crib scene, this time Portuguese, set in a golden Baroque shrine; also two very large statues of St Francis and St Clare and 16th century panels of scriptural scenes, as there are in the small Misericordia church on the other side of the main square.

An attractive village, Luz de Tavira is almost on the main road *Luz de Tavira* between Moncarapacho and Tavira. There is a great open space surrounded by low cottages in front of the large parish church, which has an enormous Renaissance doorway between Manueline pillars.

Inland from Luz de Tavira, near the village of Santo Estevão in the *Santo Estevão* Sitio de Estiramantens, is the Museu do Monte da Guerreira, a private house which the owner has made into a museum. It is open every day and the exhibits are various and of interest to those who care for furniture, pictures and china.

In lovely natural surroundings is the typical holiday village of Pedras d'el Rei. The villas, which can be rented for short or long *Pedras d'el Rei* periods, are completely equipped and very well designed. There is a reasonably priced restaurant and all the usual amenities such as a pool, clubhouse, disco, baby-sitting service, tennis, riding, a supermarket and the nearby beach of Santa Luzia, protected from the full force of the sea by a long sandy spit of land.

Lying on either side of the river Sequa, crossed by a seven-arched Roman bridge, Tavira is the prettiest town in the Algarve. On a hill *Tavira* in the centre, the castle looks down upon clean, white houses and churches. The harbour has for long been silted up and the town is cut off from the ocean by a long spit of land, but this makes bathing at Ilha de Tavira particularly safe. The water in this long arm of the sea is tidal, so there is no pollution. Over the river there are several small restaurants on the quays, which serve particularly delicious stews of chicken and clams cooked in a *cataplana*, – a kind of primitive pressure cooker consisting of two shining half moons of tin or copper which can be clamped together and placed directly on the flame. The local wine is also very good, as it is all over the Algarve. On this side of the river, too, are the Carmo church and conventual buildings, now a lyceum or grammar school. The church, though very plain outside displays wildest Baroque within; the high altar is like a scene from an opera, with beautiful 18th century chairbacked benches on either side. The key to this fantastic interior can be obtained at the cottage to the left of the church.

Cacela

Off the main road to the frontier at Vila Real de Sto Antonio, which incidentally by-passes Tavira, is the tiny settlement of the original village of Cacela, with a fort, a church and a few old cottages right on the sea. The fort is of great age, possibly on Roman foundations. It was here that Admiral Charles Napier landed the Duke of Terceira and his army, to win the Civil War between the brothers, Dom Miguel, who had usurped the throne of Portugal, and his elder brother the Emperor Dom Pedro. Inland are several tourist complexes, including the camping-bar-restaurant *Caliço*, a secluded site with a swimming pool, and the three star *Eurotel*.

Monte Gordo

Past Manta Rota, another tourist centre with a long sandy beach, is Monte Gordo. Here the pine trees reach down to the golden sands of the long wide beach which slopes steeply so swimmers are out of their depth within a few yards. There are several hotels overlooking the beach and a pretty public garden surrounding the Casino. The *Hotel Vasco da Gama* and the *Alcazar* are both four star, as is the American-operated *Albergaria Monte Gordo.* Two three star hotels, *Dos Navegadores* and *Caravelas*, and various tourist complexes, as well as large camping grounds, complete the accommodation.

Vila Real de
Sto Antonio

Vila Real is the frontier post on the broad estuary of the river Guadiana, with Ayamonte on the Spanish side. Fast ferry boats carrying cars, take about ten minutes over the crossing; they sail from either bank every half hour from 08.00 to 20.00 in the winter and from 08.00 to 23.00 in the summer.

Excursion to
Spain

This little excursion into Spain is a delightful way of spending a few hours; you just show your passport before embarking and after disembarking and there are lovely views of both towns as the ferry crosses the estuary. Customs formalities are almost non-existent, so you could buy Spanish specialities like *turrone*, that delicious sweet made of ground almonds, not unlike a super nougat, and have lunch or dinner at the *Parador Restaurante Bar*, with wide views of the river.

Vila Real is charming, laid out about 1760 by the Marques de

60

Pombal. A patterned mosaic pavement covers the whole of the central square with an elegant obelisk in the centre. The low houses are almost all plainly built but with the perfect proportions of the late 18th century which, indeed, obtained in Portugal until the beginning of this century when any country builder seemed able to produce, without the aid of any architectural plans, a building that blended harmoniously with its surroundings. The town is laid out on a grid pattern, so almost all the streets are one-way. There are some pleasant, simple restaurants along the main streets, of which *Gomes* is the best known, and there is a good camping site.

A couple of miles on the road north from Vila Real, which is the fifth and last direct route north from the Algarve to the Alentejo, stand the two fortresses of Castro Marim, which look finer from a distance than close to. The great walls of the larger of the fortresses, in reality a castle, enclose a ruined church and a small museum, containing early archaeological remains. St Sebastian's fort, by the castle, was built by King John IV, the father of Catherine of Braganza. *Castro Marim*

The winding road north passes through lovely rolling countryside. In late January and early February, the hillsides are dotted with flowering almond trees, looking like giant powder puffs, for at this time almond blossom covers most of the Algarve. The white blossoms produce sweet almonds and the pink the bitter variety. The latter are excellent for flavouring but dangerous if more than a few are eaten as they contain cyanide. The almond crop is of great importance to the economy of the Algarve, as much of it is exported. *Almond Crop*

After some 10 miles, and skirting the village of Odeleite, the road winds gradually down until a minor road to the right leads to Guerreiros do Rio, an appealing village on the Guadiana. Back to the main road where a few miles further on there is a crossing, of which the left hand goes to Perreiro and Martim Longo. The road to the right leads, in three or four miles, to Alcoutim, a lovely tiny town grouped around an early 14th century castle on a sudden bluff in the centre. The village falls down to the beautiful river with its pretty, low whitewashed houses and those of Sanlucar on the Spanish side, reflected in the calm waters of the Guadiana. There is no frontier post here, so the little skiffs and dinghies by the quay are used for fishing, while Republican guardsmen, who police the Portuguese countryside, lounge on the quayside keeping an eye on possible smugglers. *Alcoutim*

The Algarve is on the main route of birds migrating south from Europe, and even from the Arctic circle, so ornithologists can see an extraordinary variety here: dunlins, which breed in Iceland, feed on the mudflats of Portimão, bee-eaters nest in Monchique in the spring, and visitors can sometimes see large numbers perched on telegraph wires, where their blue and yellow plumage stands *Birds* out. Flocks of lovely white egrets follow the plough looking for grubs in the newly turned earth, and there are also Alpine swifts, golden orioles and the azure-winged magpies which exist only in Portugal and Spain, Japan and China. Hoopoes are abundant and on the coast there are large numbers of seabirds, including waders. Altogether about 200 different species of bird come and go in the Algarve.

Flora

The numerous varieties of wild flowers in the Algarve are at their best in February, March and April. Often, what are garden flowers in Britain – such as exceptionally tall mauve irises, geraniums, roses and, on the more arid ground towards the west, mesembryanthemum – border the sides of even main roads.

Typical street in Evora

Alentejo

One of the most beautiful parts of the country, the Alentejo is a great undulating plain which stretches from south of Setúbal to the Spanish frontier. There are forests of cork oak under which graze herds of black pigs, often tended by a solitary boy leaning on a stick and clad in one of the sheepskin caped coats characteristic of the region. The Alentejo is also the granary of Portugal and, particularly around Beja, there are great stretches of wheat. The plains are interspersed with hill towns, each with a castle at the summit encircled by a wall. In Beja and Estremoz, magnificent keeps stand guard over the plain, reflecting the fact that this part of the country was a battlefield for centuries. First, the aggressors were the Moors, who were gradually driven south until finally expelled. Then there were constant fights against the Spaniards who cast envious eyes on the fertile lands of Portugal.

For long the poorest part of the country, the provision of dams and irrigation has considerably improved the Alentejo's agriculture. Even so the long, hot, rainless summers make the cultivation of any crop impossible after late spring, apart from the rich cork   *Cork* harvest which supplies two thirds of the world's demands for the bark of the cork oak, which can be stripped only every nine years. One of the features of the cork forests is the beautiful shade of

63

reddish-brown of the trunks of newly stripped trees, which gradually turns to grey over the months.

Olive oil is another product, as the hard dry soil seems to be favourable to the growth of olive trees; and the umbrella pine yields tiny nuts from which is made pine oil with its delicious tang. Apart from these varieties of trees and the occasional eucalyptus, there are no wooded parts of the Alentejo except the foothills of the mountains separating the province from Spain. Here there are splendid groves of sweet chestnuts, walnut trees, fig trees and the Forestry Commission's plantations of conifers.

Ninety miles from Lisbon is Evora, one of the two main cities of the Alentejo, the other being Beja. Evora can be reached not only by rail from Barreiro across the river from Lisbon, but also by road from the bridge over the Tagus at Vila Franca de Xira. This road south is narrow but greatly improves and widens after the crossroads at Pegões, where the motorist must take the left turn through Vendas Novas to Montemor-o-Novo.

Montemor-o-Novo

Crowned by a castle, which can be reached by car, Montemor-o-Novo is of little interest, though it was the birthplace of St John of God (1495–1550), who devoted his life to the care of lunatics and founded the Order which bears his name and still carries on the same work. A big fair is held in this town annually on May 1st.

Just beyond Montemor, the road forks right for Evora, left for Arraiolos, Estremoz, Elvas and the upper part of the Alentejo.

Evora

One of the most interesting towns in Portugal, Evora has marvellously preserved its original layout within the encircling walls, though there has been much new building outside these ramparts. The heart of the city is the cathedral with the lovely Roman temple of Diana beside it. Also in this elegant L-shaped space is the

Accommodation

museum and the luxury *Pousada dos Loios* (tel. (0069) 24051) installed in a former convent. The bedrooms are large and comfortable, and beautifully furnished public rooms are off the cloisters, as is the restaurant, converted from the original refectory.

Temple of Diana

The 2nd century temple of Diana is the most striking of the Roman remains to be found in Portugal. The fact that the temple was for long used as a storehouse, with brick walls filling up the spaces between the fluted Corinthian pillars until the 19th century, probably ensured its present remarkable state of conservation.

Cathedral

The cathedral is essentially 12th and 13th century, though many additions have been made since then, including the later Gothic cloisters at the side, the odd conical spires, the low tower and the early 18th century chancel and high altar, built by Ludwig, the architect of Mafra. Though not beautiful as a whole, this cathedral

64

contains many features, with early polychrome statues on the side altars and good stalls in the upper choir, as well as a fine 18th century organ, recently restored by an English expert, living in Portugal, who has brought many of the early organs in Portuguese churches back to perfection.

Be sure to see the 17th century sacristy with fine furnishings and canvases. The treasury installed in the chapter house, on the opposite side of the chancel, contains ecclesiastical plate and a very unusual 13th century French ivory image of the Virgin seated with the Holy Child in her lap. The statue opens to show a triptych with high relief carvings of scenes from the life of the Virgin. The original ivory head disappeared in the 16th century and has never been found; this was when the present wooden head was put on.

The museum between the cathedral and the *Pousada dos Loios*, contains many Portuguese primitives; the most important are a whole series by Frei Carlos who was painting in Evora in the 16th century. There is also furniture and a collection of archaeological remains in the cloisters. *Museum*

A short way down from the Cathedral, the oval Praça do Geraldo, where there is a tourist office, is composed of elegant houses above arched arcades. In the intervening narrow streets, antique shops are to be found. The Praça do Geraldo is the centre of the busy life of the city, for Evora is not only a beautifully preserved town, but also an agricultural and industrial centre for the surrounding country. At one end of this Praça, is the church of Santo Antão, built in 1557. It has three formal aisles, with beautiful Baroque altars and early statues, including a rare polychrome Gothic marble group. *Praça do Geraldo*

Santo Antão

The church of São Francisco is essentially Gothic, with Renaissance and Baroque chapels. Below the church is a macabre crypt lined with human bones and skulls. *São Francisco*

The Palladian façade of the semi-ruined church of Graça is unique in Portugal, representing four gigantic figures sitting at the tops of the side pillars below two great flaming globes. *Graça*

São Braz, just outside the city walls, with a *romaria* on February 2nd, is a battlemented church with pepperpot turrets and a large square porch. This type of building is to be found elsewhere in the Alentejo, notably in Beja. *São Braz*

The recently revived University, is a complex of buildings with a large classical double cloister. Evora is particularly rich in *azulejos* and the University buildings contain 16th, 17th and 18th century tiles. Several of the rooms have painted ceilings and that of the sacristy adjoining the church has unusually good 17th century paintings of the life of Saint Ignatius, for this was at one time a Jesuit University. The charming, small Renaissance theatre is also *University* worth seeing.

Restaurants
There are several reasonable hotels and pensions in the town as well as excellent restaurants, including the *Gião*, owner-managed, in the Rua da Republica 81, and the *Arcada*, Praça do Geraldo 7, where the restaurant is reached through a café.

Charterhouse
Outside Evora are three interesting monasteries. The Charterhouse, now again inhabited by Carthusians, is beyond the Porta da Mesquita.

São Bento de Castris
São Bento de Castris is a couple of miles further on, with a big 16th century two storeyed cloister and good *azulejos*. The buildings are now used as a school. There is a *romaria* on Ascension Thursday, ten days before Pentecost.

Espinheiro
Some three miles to the north-west of Evora, is the fortified Convent of Espinheiro. It was here that Frei Carlos, the painter, lived and worked. The church has fine Renaissance and Baroque details.

Arraiolos
Evora is a good starting point from which to explore the upper Alentejo, along country roads leading from the city to Arraiolos, Estremoz and Elvas.

A castle-crowned hill town, Arraiolos has been famous for rug-making since the middle ages. These carpets are embroidered on canvas in wool and the patterns are mostly traditional, though modern, abstract and other designs are now being used.

The small well-proportioned houses shine with whitewash as do all the houses in the Alentejo, since it is a point of honour to whitewash your house at least once a year.

Quinta dos Loios
A former convent, in a valley just outside Arraiolos on the road north to Pavia and Aviz, the Quinta dos Loios is now private property and is difficult to get into. But the interior of the fortified church is well worth seeing if possible. Huge blue and white tiled panels, reaching up to the ceiling of the single-aisled edifice, include one portraying Edward the Confessor kneeling at a *prie-dieu* with his crown at his side, and a ribbon with the words in Portuguese 'Edward the Confessor, King of England'.

Compared to other parts of Portugal, there are few towns or even villages of any size in the Alentejo. Twenty miles along a lonely road to the north, Aviz seems to be a forgotten place.

Aviz
Beautifully situated on a granite escarpment above a river, with great man-made lakes stretching below, the castle of Aviz and most of the town were built in the 13th and 14th centuries. However, the very fine conventual church of St Benedict was rebuilt at the beginning of the 17th century, and the large 16th century sacristy is

66

now the oldest part of the building. The Baroque retable of the high altar is one of the best of its kind in the country. The Order of Aviz, still given as a decoration for outstanding services to Portugal, took its name from this town. The great square in front of the church and conventual buildings is singularly lovely, and the unusual *pelourinho*, or stone column, is surmounted by an eagle with widespread wings, the symbol of the town.

The road to Alter do Chão goes north-east from Aviz through beautiful country, alongside stretches of water. On the way, outside the village of Seda, there is one of the finest Roman bridges in the country. It is of great length, carried on six rounded arches, and is still in use after two thousand years.

Roman Bridge

The town of Alter is grouped around a castle on the main square. There is a white marble fountain in the square, dated 1556, with classical columns supporting a cupola over the spring.

Alter do Chão

Nearby is the great state horse breeding establishment, Estação Zóotècnica do Alter, and experimental farm, worth seeing by those interested in rare equine breeds such as the Lusitanian, which has been raised for centuries in the Iberian peninsula. Stallions are sent all over the country, horses trained and mules bred.

Crato, due north of Alter, is built on a hill crowned by a castle, and two miles to the north, are the much restored buildings of the fortified monastery of Flor da Rosa.

Crato

Portalegre

Twelve miles due east of Crato, in the foothills of the Serra de São Mamede, lies the delightful busy city of Portalegre, extremely populous in the time of the Roman occupation of Portugal, as is shown by the many contemporary roads and bridges in the environs. The museum, a former diocesan seminary by the cathedral, contains good archaeological remains, fine terracotta and other sculpture, furniture, early Arraiolos carpets, and pictures.

Museum

The cathedral has a most unusual 18th century façade, tall and wide and flanked by two towers topped by octagonal pyramids. The interior is lovely, with a groined and painted ceiling, and good canvases on the retables of the altars; the sacristy, lined with blue and white pictorial *azulejos*, contains superb vestment chests in their original condition. Shown in special glass cases is a most interesting collection of pre-Reformation English vestments. At that time, English embroidery was famous all over the Continent, and a great many examples were sent abroad. Some of these vestments can even be seen in Ponte Delgada, in the Azores. The 18th century cloister at the side of the cathedral has a unique Baroque pediment.

Cathedral

The streets going up to the top of the town are lined with rococo

houses adorned with fine ironwork balconies and there are particularly good *azulejos* in many of the houses and churches. The

Chapel of Bom Fim

small chapel of Bom Fim, on the outskirts of the town on the Castelo de Vide road, like its namesake in Setúbal, resembles a golden jewel case. Built in 1720, is still has all the original tiled panels, gilded altars and rococo frames round the canvases.

José Regio's House

The poet José Regio lived in Portalegre until his death. His house has been made into a rather touching museum of all the things that he collected during his lifetime. These mainly consist of local country art and artifacts. There are two good pensions, the *Alto Alentejo* and the *Nova* and the modern three star *Hotel D. João III.*

Castelo de Vide

Ten miles north of Portalegre, Castelo de Vide, with a Spa, is grouped around a castle which is reached through a perfect 16th century village within the outer walls. Many of the little whitewashed cottages have Gothic doors and windows. Certain of the streets and squares of this beautiful place have been un-touched since the middle ages, and the ornamental iron grilles over the windows of the 17th and 18th century houses should be noted. There are pensions and restaurants in addition to the four star *Albergaria Jardim.*

On the summit of a mountain, opposite the town, the little chapel of Senhora da Penha, glistening white in the daytime, stands out at night by the lamp which a local man lights as darkness falls in this remote spot.

Marvão

Between Castelo de Vide and the frontier post with Spain of Galegos, is the fascinating mountain-top town of Marvão. The road to the Spanish border goes below the 3,000-foot-high escarp-ment of sheer rock crowned by the battlements of the walls which surround this castellated town. Called Hermino Minor by the Romans, the tiny city is still as it was centuries ago. Reached by a hidden road winding round and up the back of the mountain, Marvão is entered through medieval archways. As can be seen from the great walls, the place has been of immense military importance through the centuries. The rough, narrow streets go between contemporary houses, many of which have been beauti-fully restored. There is the excellent *Pousada de Santa Maria* (tel. (0045) 93201), with a good restaurant. The views on all sides cover huge distances and ornithologists will be fascinated to see count-less kestrels, with sky-blue tails, which nest in the castle walls.

Medobriga

Near the road from Castelo de Vide to Marvão, are the remains of the Roman town of Medobriga near the village of Aramenha. Huge quantities of Roman remains have been found here, many of which can now be seen in the Ethnological Museum at Belem, near Lisbon.

Nisa

To the northwest of Castelo de Vide, the town of Nisa is grouped around another early castle, built at the end of the 13th century by

King Diniz, who also built the walls around the town. There is a notable Renaissance fountain, the Fonte da Pipa. Distinctive earthenware jugs and amphorae in Roman shapes are made here, often with small pebbles set in patterns in the soft clay before firing.

Due north of Nisa, the river Tagus, still wide although so near the Spanish frontier, enters a gorge, the Portas de Rodão. The towering cliffs on either side are worn into fantastic shapes and it was here that Wellington took his forces across the river in May 1811, during the Peninsular War, to join Beresford for one of his famous pincer movements. The river is crossed by a bridge, leading to Castelo Branco and the Serra da Estrela.

Portas de Rodão

The roads out of Portalegre towards Spain go through wooded country, in the foothills of the Serra de São Mamede. In the village of Reguengo, a road leads to Alegrete, another tiny fortified frontier town. The little village within the outer walls of the castle, is brilliant with flowering plants which form an enchanting composition with the beautifully proportioned doors and windows.

Alegrete

A large agricultural centre, Campo Maior played a leading part in the wars between Portugal and Spain, as it did in the Peninsular War. Beresford was named Marquis of Campo Maior by the Portuguese after the successful expulsion of the French troops. The castle has many 17th century additions to the original early 14th century building.

Campo Maior

The frontier town of Ougela, five miles north-east of Campo Maior, is worth seeing by those interested in remote places. The road goes through high, lonely country, covered with cistus and wild lavender in the spring, hawks wheeling overhead, till the walls of Ougela come into view. The road ends at the medieval settlement on a low hill surrounded by the castle walls. Entry is through a double postern and the visitor walks up into a great open space, the size of a cricket field, surrounded by low cottages; a fine, ruined house with a nobleman's coat of arms above the gaping door and the castle tower to one side. The people sit at their doors chatting and preparing the midday meal on charcoal braziers for their menfolk coming in from the fields below and for their children, whose modern school is one of the few buildings outside the walls.

Ougela

Three miles south of Campo Maior, at Castro de Segovia, are the remains of one of the most important Iron Age settlements in the south of Portugal. This early fortification covers an elongated eminence, particularly suitable for defence as it overlooks the surrounding plain. Recent excavations have shown three distinct periods of habitations, constructed of small blocks of stone without any mortar. Pottery, glass, jewellery, buckles, pins and bronze coins have been found.

Castro de Segovia

Elvas

Ten miles south of Campo Maior lies the large walled city of Elvas, standing on a vast mound jutting up from the plain. The view over the city from this road is particularly beautiful. There has been much building outside the walls, including the *Pousada* of *Santa Luzia* (tel. (091) 22194), with a notable restaurant. But by far the greater number of the 15,000 inhabitants still live in the old houses along the narrow streets rising up to the castle keep. The place is filled with soldiers as the city is still one of the chief garrisons of the country for, owing to its position, it was involved not only in the Peninsular War but also, like Campo Maior, in the wars with Spain.

Museum There is a delightful museum which includes, not only some interesting 18th century portraits, but also local pottery and oddities, like the first typewriter and the first sewing machine to reach the city. The churches contain fine *azulejos* and many have Baroque features.

Cathedral The parish church, formerly the cathedral when the city was a bishopric, is fundamentally a Manueline building, with a particularly fine 18th century organ. The sacristy has a lovely painted ceiling and good fittings. The square in front of the church is paved in a most unusual black and white checkerboard pattern.

Freiras de On the way up to the castle from here, is the strange and exciting
São Domingos church of the Freiras de São Domingos, built in 1543. The octagonal interior is elegantly beautiful, the cupola supported on eight columns painted with gold and coloured formal flowers and arabesques as are the rounded arches between them. The walls are lined with carpet tiles of 1659. The church is lit only by a lantern in the cupola and two small windows, and the resulting semi-darkness gives a curious, almost mosque-like feeling to the place.

Aqueduct To the south of the city, the immense five-tiered aqueduct strides across the plain. This was built on Roman foundations and took from 1498 to 1622 to complete. The people of Elvas were forced to pay a levy to finance this huge undertaking. The *Estalagem D. Sancho II* is four star and in the city, the *Hotel D. Luis* is three star.

Juromenha South of Elvas on the way to Alandroal and built within castle walls, Juromenha overlooks the broad valley of the river Guadiana which here forms the frontier with Spain.

Alandroal The towers of the castle of Alandroal, a foundation of the Order of Aviz, and the walls surrounding the small town, have been beautifully restored; the whole place, including the houses outside the walls, is a most elegant ensemble.

Redondo South-west of Alandroal, Redondo contains many delightful buildings. In addition to the tall towered castle, the Casa da Rede is a lovely 18th century country house with strange griffin-topped portals. The 15th century Misericordia church inside the castle, has a Manueline choir, a painted roof, 18th century tiled panels and lovely Baroque retables, while beautiful iron work decorates the windows and balconies of many of the houses, particularly in the

70

Rua de São Miguel.

The road north from Redondo to Estremoz goes by the Serra de Ossa. The convent of St Paul the Hermit, scene of a big gathering of all the surrounding people on Ascension Thursday, is a Baroque building with splendid 18th century *azulejos* in the church. Catherine of Braganza, wife of Charles II, stayed here in 1699 after she had returned to Portugal as a widow. In the next century, it was the place of exile of the Meninos de Palhava, the illegitimate half-brothers of King John V, whose beautiful palace in Lisbon is now the Spanish Embassy; their painted carriage, in the Coach Museum at Belem, has a royal crown slightly askew on the roof.

There are dolmens all over this northern part of the Alentejo and on the southern slopes of the Serra de Ossa, near the tiny village of Nossa Senhora do Freixo, is a large group with other neolithic remains.

Estremoz

This is one of the most delightful towns in the Alentejo, halfway between Arraiolos and Elvas. Large and prosperous, the luxury *Pousada da Rainha Santa Isabel* (tel. (0061) 22618), is installed in the palace adjacent to the castle. The room in which Queen Isabel, who became St Elizabeth of Portugal, died in 1336, was later transformed into a tiny chapel with *azulejos* and frescoes of her life, including one of the Miracle of the Roses when the Queen, carrying alms to the poor, was surprised by her husband King Diniz, and opened the folds of her skirt to reveal only roses.

The splendid keep stands at the summit of the hill up which the medieval town is built. From the top of this keep, there is an amazing view as far as Palmela, just south of Lisbon, Marvão to the east, and even, on fine days, the mountains of the Serra de Estrela to the north. In the *largo* is the great church of Santa Maria, built in the 16th century on the site of a Mosque; the noble interior has three aisles and is almost square.

The centre of the lower part of the town, within 17th century ramparts, is the spacious Rossio. A big weekly fair is held here on Saturdays, when the local earthenware still made in Roman and Etruscan shapes, is on sale, as are small painted earthenware religious figures for Christmas cribs and others clad in local costumes. In this square is the *Hotel Alentejano*, a good inexpensive commercial hotel, serving breakfast only; there are several excellent restaurants above the cafés. On the side opposite the hotel, the regional museum shows models of local crafts and costumes. The town hall is in a fine old convent with beautiful *azulejo* panels of the life of Saint Philip Neri up the staircase.

Other notable and rare glazed tiles are those of the huge panels of the War of Independence against Spain in the 17th century Palacio

Tocha, in the Largo D. José. The convent of São Francisco, now a cavalry barracks, has a stairway frieze of tiles of delicate pink, yellow and green ribbons and garlands between slender vases. The Gothic church adjoining can be entered from the street and contains a 17th century Tree of Jesse and the tomb of Vasco Esteves Gato, his bearded head resting on three pillows and his feet on two dogs.

Vieros

On the road to Monforte, which is halfway between Estremoz and Portalegre, Vieros is grouped around a castle, with an Iron Age fort a mile to the south.

Monforte

The castellated town of Monforte has elegant houses, churches with good *azulejos* and, at Torre de Palma some three miles away, is a Roman town which has been largely excavated. The mosaics include a particularly fine one with five prancing horses and mosaics of mythological figures. An early Christian basilica is on the periphery and its three aisles and baptistry can still be traced.

Borba

Around ten miles to the east of Estremoz, on the Elvas road, the town of Borba is known for its excellent wine with a slightly metallic taste. Being in the centre of marble quarries, the doorways, steps and window frames of even the humblest cottage, are made of the local marble. The streets of this small town are lined with antique shops, and a museum of crucifixes of all dates and from a great number of places, has recently been opened.

Vila Viçosa

A few miles to the south-east of Borba is the royal town of Vila Viçosa, once the seat of the dukes of Braganza, who became monarchs of Portugal after the Restoration in 1640.

Chase

The Braganza Chase, or *tapada*, the largest enclosed space in the country, is surrounded by walls almost 12 miles in length. The Chase is full of game and has become a reserve for wild animals.

Ducal Palace

The Ducal Palace, its great façade of creamy marble, coloured in places to a warm gold, with three storeys of perfectly proportioned windows, fills the entire west side of the main square. The interior, open to the public, contains many of the possessions of the last King of Portugal, who left all his estates and belongings to his own country, when he died in exile in England in 1932. So, mixed up with splendid tapestries, furniture, pictures and marvellous Continental porcelain, there are Victorian and Edwardian pieces and watercolours by King Carlos I, who was assassinated in Lisbon in 1908 on his return from a visit to this palace. There is also a small collection of coaches, carriages and arms and the old kitchen is

Archaeological Museum
Augustine Church

filled with shining copper pots and pans. At one side of the Palace Square are the ruins of the castle in which an archaeological museum has been installed. Opposite the palace the Agostinhos church is a satisfying, sober building in which are splendid 17th

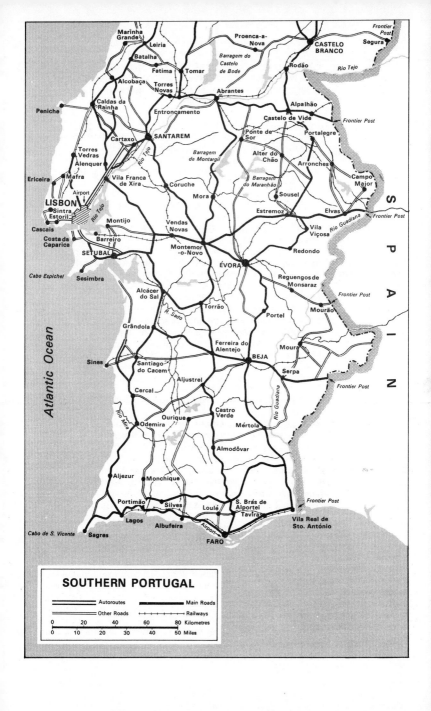

SOUTHERN PORTUGAL

══════ Autoroutes	▬▬▬▬ Main Roads
══════ Other Roads	+++++ Railways

0   20   40   60   80 Kilometres
0   10   20   30   40   50 Miles

century Braganza tombs all resting on the backs of coal-black lions.

Chagas
Convent
On the south side of the square, the Chagas Convent is a Renaissance building made extremely attractive by roofs at many different levels. The cloister is charming and the church contains an early 16th century Flemish triptych.

Horse Fair
Between the town and the railway station, the huge Campo da Restauraçao is the scene, in August, of one of the biggest horse fairs in the Alentejo. Lines of picketed horses, mules and donkeys, all with shining coats, cover the great space. The town is then alive with gypsies and an amusement fair is set up with roundabouts and coconutshies.

Evoramonte

Convention of
1834
A few miles out of Estremoz, on the Lisbon road, a fork to the left, signposted Evora, goes under the unusual village and square castle of Evoramonte. On a high hill, this castle has recently been entirely restored. The great bastion-like mass can be seen for miles along the road between Arraiolos and Estremoz and, as can be imagined, the view from the top stretches all over this part of the Alentejo. It was here that the Convention was signed in 1834 which ended the Civil War between the two brothers, Pedro IV, who had become Emperor of Brazil, and Miguel I, who was then compelled to abdicate in favour of his niece, Maria II. The village alongside the Castle is enchanting and has the smallest Misericordia in Portugal, with a tiny chapel lined with blue and white tiled panels of the Works of Mercy, at the side of the little hospital, which is now a hospice for the aged. The only street, lined with low whitewashed houses, bright with flowers pouring from window boxes and earthenware pots, leads to the Gothic parish church.

Mourão
A road south-east of Evora leads to Reguengos and Mourão, the last town before the frontier post with Spain at São Leonardo. Mourão is dominated by the keep of the castle, the fortifications of which were much altered by Vauban in the late 17th century.

Monsaraz
A side road from Reguengos leads to Monsaraz, another fortified border town, but small in size, which, after being captured from the Moors by D. Afonso Henriques, was presented to the Templars. The entrance is through an ogival archway and at the other end of the single street, is the keep above more Vaubanesque fortifications. There are lovely old houses in the small square with the town hall on the south side. Some of the houses are ornamented with secular frescoes, very rare in this country. The large, almost square, parish church is not unlike that at Estremoz, already described. The three aisles are supported on heavy stone pillars and there are fine Baroque altars. Through the sacristy is a tiny museum with church vessels and curiosities of the region.

Beja

The main city of the southern part of the Alentejo is Beja. The

74

reputed author of the *Love Letters of a Portuguese Nun*, lived in the Convento da Conceição, now a museum. These letters, translated from the French soon after their first publication in 1669, remain a fascinating literary mystery. The Portuguese originals, if they ever existed, have never been discovered; the nun who wrote them to a French officer, has been identified with a Soror Mariana Alcoforado. It is known that this nun was living in the convent at the right period, and she ended her long life as Sister Portress. These letters are believed to have inspired Elizabeth Barrett Browning's 'Sonnets from the Portuguese'.

Love Letters of a Portuguese Nun

The convent is curious rather than beautiful. The wide pointed arches of the façade support a highly decorated Gothic balustrade. The interior, chapter house, cloister and galleries are all lined with early *azulejos*, They house rare canvases, a Ming ceramic bowl with the arms of Pêrro de Faria, who returned from the Far East in 1541, and church vessels and vestments. Among the archaeological remains from the surrounding region, are fine Roman mosaics and coins, and the Visigothic collection is one of the largest in the country. The chapel, with the wildest of Baroque decoration and large *azulejo* panels, is also shown.

Convent of the Conception

In the Largo do Porvir, near the Conceição, is the strange adobe-like Church of Santa Maria. It could be in Mexico, with heavy, low plastered columns intersected by Gothic arches leading in to the narthex. The classical interior has Baroque altars and a Tree of Jesse in a chapel to the left of the nave.

Santa Maria

The impressive castle keep, built by King Diniz in 1310, has a most elegant double row of battlements, but, with its surrounding walls, is all that now remains of the medieval fortifications which, in the 18th century, still had 40 towers. The top of the keep is reached by a corkscrew staircase, only recommended to the young and energetic, but there is a superb view from the top.

Castle

Beja has several restaurants but no hotel, only three pensions, the *Rocha*, *O Lidador* and *Tomás*.

One of the roads to Beja, from Lisbon, turns left in the charming town of Alcaçer do Sal. Falling down to the river Sado, glistening whitewashed houses stand out against the stones of the ruined castle, on which myriads of storks nest in the spring. The strange clacking sound of their beaks fills the air, as the huge ungainly birds circle around.

Alcaçer do Sal

Storks

The café restaurants by the river are all good and the *Estalagem Herdade da Barrosinha*, a mile to the east, has pleasant rooms and a restaurant.

The *Pousada de Vale de Gaio* (tel. (065) 66100), designed mainly for sportsmen, is by a man-made lake of the same name on the way to Beja.

Alcaçovas	North-west of Beja is a group of interesting small towns. Alcaçovas contains early town houses, including that of the Barahonas with pyramid towers at the corners, and that of the Condes de Alcaço-vas, which retains many of the original 15th century Gothic features. Outside the town to the west, the Convent of Esperança contains unusual blue, yellow and white *azulejos* depicting trees, bulls and lions.
Viana do Alentejo *Nossa Senhora de Aires*	South-east of Alcaçovas, Viana do Alentejo lies around a castle; the flying-buttressed parish church is built up inside the south-east wall. Pepperpot turrets stud the double row of battlements. Near the town, there is a big *romaria* to the 18th century pilgrimage church of Nossa Senhora de Aires, on the fourth Sunday of September. In the chancel of the church, a golden baldachino, surmounted by a crown, towers above the altar. The fair outside has a number of booths selling all manner of country wares, while mules and horses for sale are led around by gypsies, of which remarkable nomadic people there are many in the Alentejo.
Portel	Some 15 miles due east of Viana do Alentejo, Portel is reached by a good road going through the wide cultivated lands of this part of the province. Flocks of egrets follow the plough, their shining white plumage showing up against the earth as they alight to pick up the grubs turned over by the blades. The castle, shut on Sundays, is a noble building surrounded by high battlemented walls with towers and a keep.
Vera Cruz de Marmelar *Knights of Malta*	A small village to the east, Vera Cruz de Marmelar, is of interest as the first foundation of the Order of Malta in Portugal. Portraits of the members of this Order surround the nave of the church, far too big for the small settlement surrounding it. In the church is venerated the earliest relic of the Holy Cross in Portugal, brought here by the Knights of Malta in the time of King Diniz (1282), and historically documented since then. The relic is preserved in an ornate filigree reliquary made in the early 18th century.
Alvito	South of Viana do Alentejo, Alvito is dominated by a large, late 15th century fortified house. The rectangular plan, with round towers, looks like a castle but it has always been a private dwelling. The much-restored parish church contains fine carpet patterned *azulejos* and there is a charming small museum of sacred art in the secularized church of Nossa Senhora das Neves.
Santiago do Cacém *Miróbriga*	Almost 50 miles due west of Beja towards the Atlantic, Santiago do Cacem, with the *Pousada de São Tiago* (tel. (0017) 22459), is grouped below a castle built by the Templars. The dark shapes of cypresses stand up above the grey battlemented walls now surrounding the local cemetery. The path which goes right round, under the walls and towers, gives wide views over the town and countryside. On the outskirts, the Roman city of Miróbriga is being excavated and contains the only Roman circus yet to be found in the country.

76

On the coast, beyond Santiago, is the town of Sines, birthplace of the great discoverer Vasco da Gama. The archaeological museum, in a private house, possesses extraordinary early jewellery, excavated near the property of Gaio in 1966. A vast oil terminal is now being constructed at Sines, and the supporting infrastructures can be seen for many miles inland.

Sines

Due south of Sines, via Cercal, lies Vila Nova de Milfontes on the estuary of the Mira river. Just above the town a bridge leading to the Algarve crosses the river. The small place and the estuary are lovely, with low hills flanking the usually placid waters. A small ruined castle guarding the point has been restored by Dom Luis d'Almeida and made into a delightful guest house. The 12 double rooms all have private bathrooms and visitors feel that they are guests in a beautifully run private house, for Dom Luis presides at the long refectory table where excellent meals are served.

Vila Nova de Milfontes

East of Beja, over one of the few bridges crossing the river Guadiana, is another castellated city, Serpa, with the *Pousada de São Gens*, Alto de São Gens (tel. (0079) 52327), just outside. The city is entered by medieval gateways and contains adobe-like churches. It is the centre of a district devoted to polyphonic singing which, sung by groups of country people, can sometimes be heard in the streets and lanes or even in a café.

Serpa

Two roads out of Serpa lead to Moura. This place, also near the Guadiana, has a Spa which sends bottled water all over the country. The castle, with a keep, was originally built by the Moors and has been reconstructed in the intervening centuries. Many of the houses have strangely shaped, decorated chimneys and in the main square, by the parish church of St John the Baptist, with a Manueline portal, there is an elegant Regency marble fountain.

Moura

Due east of Moura, the remote town of Barrancos is approached through marvellous deserted countryside, bright with wild flowers in the spring, in the summer burnt to a wonderful pale umber colour. The people here speak a kind of patois – a mixture of Portuguese and Spanish. Just before the town is reached, an unmetalled narrow road leads north to the frontier castle of Noudar, with ruined houses grouped around the tower, for now no one lives in this isolated place. There is a frontier post with Spain at Rosal de la Frontera, east of Serpa.

Barrancos

Noudar

Twenty-five miles south-east of Beja, Mertola is another ancient town on the banks of the Guadiana, here again crossed by a bridge. The castle keep was built in 1292 by the first Master of the Order of São Tiago. The five-aisled parish church, unique in Portugal, is square in shape and was undoubtedly a mosque for there is an unmistakable *Mihrab* at one side. Big fairs are held from time to time and there are excellent simple restaurants, including the *Alengarve* in the Rua Dr Afonso Costa. From here goes the most easterly of the five roads from the Alentejo into the Algarve.

Mertola

Nazaré

Estremadura

This long stretch of country lies between the river Tagus and the Atlantic ocean, north of Lisbon up to Leiria, east to Abrantes and for practical purposes, a small section, the Ribatejo, south of the Tagus. Estremadura includes many places of the greatest interest – Santarem, Obidos, the Monasteries of Alcobaça, Batalha, and Tomar, the seat of the Templars in Portugal, as well as the pilgrimage shrine of Fatima. The country is fertile and closely planted with vines and vegetables. The few ranges of hills look higher than they really are, owing to the surrounding flattish countryside. North of Ericeira, a road leads past several small beaches until a turn inland reaches Torres Vedras.

Lines of Torres Vedras

Torres Vedras gives its name to the famous Lines which were constructed, mainly by Portuguese workers, under the direction of Wellington, during the Peninsular War. Just above the town, on a hill adjacent to that of the castle, is a carefully reconstructed fort in which those interested in military affairs or in the Peninsular War, can see how the fortifications were planned. This first Line consists of a number of redoubts on the summits of the hills, which stretch over to the Tagus just below Vila Franca de Xira, thus protecting the wedge-shaped peninsula on which Lisbon is situated.

Torres Vedras

Torres Vedras is large and busy, and accessible by rail and buses. Good restaurants are the *Solar*, Rua Gago Countinho 13, *Barrete Preto*, Rua Paiva de Andrade 27 and *O Fernando*, Travessa José Eduardo Cesar 5. There is no hotel however. The town possesses a small museum in which Roman remains and early sculpture occupy the ground floor. Upstairs is a fine series of religious primitive paintings from a church by the castle, Chinese porcelain and an unusual series of late 16th century tiled panels with animals, including a dromedary and a leopard, in a sylvan background.

This beautiful church is at the entrance to the town by a public garden. The 17th and 18th century painted statues are memorable and in the cloisters, walled off long ago to make Municipal offices, are interesting early 18th century *azulejo* panels, one showing an elephant and others the long winding funeral procession of São Gonçalo de Lagos whose tomb is in the church.

Graça Church

About two miles to the south-west of Torres Vedras, at Zambujal, are the remains of one of the most complex fortified prehistoric settlements of the whole Iberian peninsula.

Prehistoric Settlement

The Castro de Zambujal, though largely destroyed over the centuries to provide stone for local building, is still of the greatest interest, and the whole plan of the Castro can be traced. The copper and iron artifacts and other objects excavated here, indicate that Zambujal must have had its origins in a race of people from the central and eastern Mediterranean who came to prospect for copper and other metals, between 3,000 BC and 2,500 BC.

Other very early remains are to be found within a few miles of Torres Vedras, among them an Iron Age settlement with an oval fortress at Povoadao; on the summit of an escarpment of rock surmounting the Pena hill by a village called Varro, there are several funerary chambers.

Iron Age Settlement

The road south from Torres Vedras to Mafra, passes the elegant village of Turcifal. A by-pass now goes round it, but it is worth driving down the main street, past the huge 18th century church which was built from marble and stone left over from the monastery at Mafra. In the sacristy is a rare English Queen Anne chinoiserie long-case clock, with the original works. There is an unusual number of these English grandfather clocks in Portugal, not only in the sacristies of many churches but also in houses and Government offices, because the Marquis of Pombal, the Prime Minister who rebuilt those parts of Lisbon destroyed in the earthquake of 1755, ordered a whole shipload from England. Lovely 18th century houses with fine ironwork on the balconies and lower windows, line the village street.

Turcifal

North-west of Torres Vedras, towards the sea, the Spa of Vimeiro is

Vimeiro

particularly good for kidney and liver complaints. There are two excellent hotels, one, the *Porto Novo*, on the beach nearby, as well as a nine-hole golf course.

Battle of
Vimeiro
The Battle of Vimeiro was actually fought near the village of Maceira on August 21st 1808, when Wellington, commanding English and Portuguese troops, beat the French, commanded by Junot. There is a monument on the site to record the event.

Lourinhã
It is a curious fact that few country roads in Portugal go near the sea, and that north from Torres Vedras to Peniche is no exception. The way goes through Lourinhã, with a castle standing high over the small town, near which is the sandy expanse of the Praia de Areia Branca, with a camping ground and several restaurants.

Peniche

Surfing
Peniche, a big fishing port, has an impregnable fortress on the Cape, long used as a prison. There are strange rock formations and deep caves in the surrounding cliffs and the sea, with its great Atlantic waves, is particularly suitable for surfing, though not for ordinary swimming. Peniche has a couple of simple pensions and several restaurants.

Berlenga
Islands

Youth Hostel
A motorboat leaves Peniche every morning for the Berlenga Islands, which lie about eight miles out to sea. The crossing can be very rough as there is a 'race' in the comparatively narrow channel between the islands and the land. There are two main islands, Berlenga Grande and Berlenga Pequena. The former, roughly a square mile in size, is surrounded by high cliffs on which there is a lighthouse and a few fishermen's cottages. The only landing place is by the fort of São João Baptista, which juts into the sea from a narrow causeway. This fort is now a Youth Hostel and many young people go there in the summer months, taking their own bedding and provisions. Small motorboats can be hired to take visitors round the watery caves, some of which have been compared with the grottoes in Capri. The grassy, treeless summit of the island is reached by a long flight of steps, cut into the sloping cliffs above the landing place. It is covered with wild flowers in the spring, and there is a strange type of wild black rabbit which breeds there.

Atouguia da
Baleia
The road east through Peniche to Obidos, passes the village of Atouguia da Baleia. This was an important place in the Middle Ages and a small Gothic fountain, like a tiny castle stands in the principal square. The parish church contains primitive paintings and a beautiful 14th century relief stone carving of the Nativity.

Serra d'El Rei
An even smaller village, near Atouguia, is Serra d'El Rei with the remains of a 14th century royal palace along the main street. There are Gothic windows, doors and ceilings and part of it has been made into a private house.

Obidos

The completely walled town of Obidos is one of the showplaces of

Portugal. The main entrance from the road that runs north beneath the town, is by a covered double gateway with pictorial *azulejos* surrounding a balcony. The main street leads through white-washed houses, geraniums falling from every window box, to the many-towered castle at the other end. A small luxury *pousada* (tel. (062) 95105) has been installed in the castle, with a restaurant open to visitors. The top of the wide encircling walls can be reached by several flights of steps, and it is worth walking round them to see the delightful conglomeration of buildings and narrow streets below, while the battlemented outer side of this walk gives on to marvellous views all round. The streets still have their medieval paving of large, flat stones and are broken at intervals by small *largos*, or squares, with stone benches on which visitors can rest or picnic. The *Estalagem do Convento* and the *Mansão de Torre*, both four star, are excellent.

Castle

The museum, open from 10.00 to 13.00 and 14.00 to 17.00, closed on Sundays, was set up with the cooperation of the Gulbenkian Foundation, and has some lovely things in it, including four entrancing 18th century angels in wood and three small paintings on copper of the same period. A special gallery contains the Peninsular War collection formed by Frederico Pinto Basto. This includes arms, drums and maps, among them a fascinating high relief map of the whole of the Lines of Torres Vedras.

Museum

The parish church of Santa Maria (closed from 13.00 to 14.00), by the museum, is worth seeing. The walls are lined with unusual blue and white *azulejos* in large swirling patterns, right up to the ceiling which is painted with negro figures, flowers, arabesques and foliage in all colours. The most interesting paintings in the church are by Josefa of Obidos, in the retable of a side chapel. This 17th century woman painter, is as well known for her still lifes as for her religious canvases. The daughter of a local man and a woman from Seville, Josefa was only 50 when she died, but it is known that she not only painted in oils but was also a miniaturist, an etcher, a modeller in terracotta, a calligrapher and worked in silver, in addition to having many pupils in her studio. Little known outside Portugal, this painter is one of the few known women artists of the 17th century, and might well repay further study.

Santa Maria Church

The Lagoa de Obidos, a large brackish lagoon, is usually cut off from the sea by a sandbank which is opened at intervals to let in fresh sea water. Low hills and moors fall down to the shore and boats can be taken from Foz do Arelho for excursions on this great stretch of water, containing several varieties of fish but, unfortunately, gradually silting up.

Lagoa de Obidos

Boating

A few miles north of Obidos, a secondary road comes to Caldas da Rainha, a Spa famous for treatment of rheumatism, with a large hospital, founded by Queen Leonor in the 15th century.

Caldas da Rainha

The main square of the town has a colourful open-air market every

Market

morning, selling not only fruit and vegetables but also clothing, baskets and other locally-made goods. Several of the many good restaurants in Caldas are located on this square.

Pottery

Caldas is famous for its large pottery factories; much of the ware is a beautiful off-white and the leaf dishes are particularly effective in bright green. This earthenware is on sale in numberless shops

José Malhoa Museum

between the main square and the large park, in which is the José Malhoa Museum, containing mainly late 19th and early 20th century paintings and sculptures.

North of Caldas lie two of Portugal's most famous buildings, the Abbeys of Alcobaça and Batalha. The road passes through lovely,

Alfeizarão

hilly country. In the village of Alfeizarão, famous for the local sponge cakes, a turning to the west leads to the watering place of

São Martinho do Porto

São Martinho do Porto, wonderful for young children as it lies on an almost completely landlocked stretch of water with a sandy beach all around. There is a Youth Hostel, the four star *Estalagem da Concha* and the two star *Hotel do Parque*.

Alcobaça

The great monastery of Santa Maria in Alcobaça, which fills one side of the main square, was a Cistercian foundation and the plan is very similar to those of foundations of the same Order in France. The three aisles are all of the same height and the vista of immensely tall honey-coloured columns, stretches away into the distance, in what is the largest church in the country.

In the transept are the highly decorated 14th century Gothic tombs of Dom Pedro I and his mistress Inez de Castro, facing each other so that their first sight would be of each other's beloved form on the Last Day. The right-hand transept contains a remarkable late 17th century painted terracotta life-size group of the death of St Bernard. A vestibule, this side of the church, behind the high altar, leads to the sacristy with a crazy Manueline portal. At the end of the large room, is a superb almost circular, relic chapel. The golden niches are occupied by figures and busts of Saints.

Chapter House

A door in the left hand transept leads to a double cloister, off which is the great chapter house with huge standing terracotta statues of saints and angels. Further along is the famous kitchen, lined with pale washed-grey tiles, with a huge, hooded open fireplace in the centre and under the windows, a fish tank with a stream running

Refectory

through it. Next door is the immense refectory, for at its zenith this monastery housed several hundred monks, and judging from the size of this great dining room and the kitchen, they could all sit down and eat at the same time.

Sala dos Reis

The Sala dos Reis is also entered through the cloisters. Round this whitewashed room are busts and statues of Portuguese kings clad in 18th century dress, and at one end, a large panel of 18th century manuscript *azulejos*, describing the history of the monastery. In one corner stands a bronze soup tureen of heroic size which is said to have been used for the making of the soldiers' soup at the Battle of Aljubarrota in 1385, when invading Spaniards were once more driven out of the country. Three pensions, the *Bau*, *Mosteiro* and *Corações Unidos* are all in or near the main square.

West of Alcobaça is the fishing port of Nazaré. The local people are believed to descend from the Phoenicians and many are grey-eyed with noticeably fine straight noses like those of profiles on Etruscan vases. They clung to their own strange form of dress for far longer than any other community in Portugal. Indeed, some of the men still wear bright coloured wool tartan trousers, with brilliant shirts, often patched in different shades and some of the women wear black shawls and full skirts over many layers of startlingly white petticoats trimmed with lace.

Nazaré

The men go out fishing in long narrow boats, peculiar to this part of the coast; the prows, with an eye painted on either side, terminating in a high point. The ocean is dangerous and in the winter the Atlantic gales drive straight into the bay, so fishing is given up and the boats are hauled from the beach into the streets and squares. Long ago the boats, filled with their catch, were dragged up the beach by pairs of oxen, now the more practical but less romantic tractor, does the same work. The Hotels *Nazaré* and *Praia* are both three star, the *Dom Fuas*, two star and there are several good pensions and restaurants.

Fishing

Above the town, to the north, at the top of a high cliff reached by a funicular as well as by road, is the Sitio quarter. Pretty low houses surround a wide space and at one side of the late 17th century Baroque church, are the remains of a royal palace. The church of Our Lady of Nazareth is beautiful, with fine sculptures, *azulejo* panels of scenes of the Old Testament and a golden high altar. Opposite, on the cliff top, is the tiny chapel built on the site of the legendary apparition of the Virgin Mary to Dom Fuas Rupinho in 1182, to save him and his horse from plunging to their deaths over the cliff edge, when he was chasing the devil who had taken the form of a stag.

Sitio

Lovers of the rococo should go a few miles off the road between Nazaré and Alcobaça, to the wonderfully untouched Bernadine monastery of Santa Maria da Coz. Little remains of the actual buildings of the monastery at Coz as they were pillaged in the past for building in the village. The plain, austere exterior of the great church, gives no indication of the extraordinary riches within. The late 17th, early 18th century woodwork is in its original state, as are the beautiful polychrome statues. The coffered ceiling is painted with allegorical figures set among flowers and seraphim. The nuns' choir, separated from the church by a gilded grille, also has a painted ceiling and a much earlier Manueline door at the end.

Coz

The road from Alcobaça to Batalha passes the village of Aljubarrota, scene of the great battle of August 14th, 1385, when John I beat

Aljubarrota

the Castilians, and somewhat further on the chapel of São Jorge de Aljubarrota marks the spot where the Constable, Nuno Alvares Pereira, raised his standard before the battle. The pleasant *Estalagem do Cruzeiro* is on this road.

Porto de Mós

A turning to the right goes to Porto de Mós, with a completely restored 13th century castle on a hill rising abruptly from the town. The view of the hills rolling away towards Fatima in the east, and the plain to the sea in the west, is particularly satisfying. The castle, with its bright green roof, looks eerily like a child's construction.

Batalha

The second of Portugal's most famous abbeys, the Monastery of Our Lady of Victory at Batalha, was started by King John I in 1388 in fulfilment of a vow he made before the Battle of Aljubarrota. Unlike the honey-coloured Alcobaça, the interior of Batalha is dark and grey in feeling, and resembles many of the great Gothic cathedrals of England and of France. However, it possesses several features that are uniquely Portuguese. The square Founder's Chapel to the right on entering the high nave, was built as the resting place of King John and his English Queen, Philippa of Lancaster. Their two figures, eyes wide open and hand in hand, lie on top of the heavy sarcophagus while in niches, round the walls, are the tombs of six of their sons, including that of Henry the Navigator.

Royal Cloister

On the other side of the church, which is one of the few ecclesiastical buildings in Portugal with stained glass in the windows, a door leads to the exuberantly Manueline Royal Cloister. Earlier, and therefore more Gothic in feeling than that at Jeronimos near Lisbon, it is a single storeyed building.

Chapter House

Off this cloister is the chapter house, each side of which is 70 ft in length. The great fan-vaulted roof springs from low columns set against the walls and is so large that one is amazed at the skill with which the medieval builders calculated the stresses so that no further support was necessary.

Unknown Soldiers

A soldier always stands on guard in this chapter house over the tombs of Portugal's two unknown soldiers killed during World War I, when the Portuguese sent an Expeditionary Force to France to fight alongside their ancient allies, the British. In this force were soldiers from the Portuguese mainland and from the then overseas provinces in Africa, hence the two tombs.

Cloister of Dom Afonso

The cloister of Dom Afonso lies just beyond, with a plainly-columned second storey set above the Gothic arches of the lower. It is simpler and, in some ways, more attractive than the Royal Cloister. The clipped box hedges in both cloisters scent the air with their delicious spicy smell.

Unfinished Chapels

The *Capelas Imperfeitas*, or Unfinished Chapels, are the oddest of the diverse architectural features of Batalha. Their truncated columns rise into the air at the back of the apse. This miracle of

84

intricately carved stonework, cannot be reached from inside the church but through a small door in the exterior at the north-east end. The octagonal building, open to the sky, was begun by Dom Duarte in 1435 as a pantheon for himself, but he died three years later and they were only resumed by King Manuel, who gave his name to the specialised form of decorated Gothic which is here shown at its most exuberant. It is fortunate that the oriental-like complexities of the carving over the great portal and surrounding the seven radial chapels, have not been more injured by the sun and rain of over 500 years, and they remain one of the strangest manifestations of human imagination.

It is a disaster that this great building should have been dwarfed by the construction, in recent years, of motorways above and around it. The charming little 18th century houses, almost nestling up to the great walls, have been swept away, and the fact that they have been replaced by an equestrian statue of Nuno Alvares Pereira in the great open space, modern shops and the excellent five star *Estalagem do Mestre Dom Afonso Domingues*, makes no recompense for the former setting which enhanced the impact of the Abbey instead of diminishing it.

For non-drivers, there are plenty of local buses in the area.

Leiria

North of Batalha, on the main road to Coimbra and Oporto, Leiria has been by-passed, but from this road there is such a splendid view of Leiria's great castle, crowning an almost perpendicular rock, that most travellers would wish to turn aside and see the city which can boast of such a citadel. Leiria is grouped on either side of the river Liz, surrounded with gardens and open spaces leading to an arcaded square, in which are several cafés with tables set out under the arches. The *Estalagem Claras* is four star, the *Euro-Sol* three star and the homely *Lis*, two star.

A little to the north is the Renaissance cathedral and at the side a small country museum containing medals and coins, furniture, paintings, carpets and church vessels. *Museum*

The castle is the most dramatically situated in the whole of Portugal. A road winds up to the gate, flanked by two crenellated towers, and a stairway on the left leads to the centre of the castle. The keep stands high above the remains of the Gothic chapel of Our Lady of Pena and the royal palace. A staircase leads to the upper storeys of this 14th century palace, which was built and lived in by King Diniz and his Queen. Several rooms in the building remain, in addition to a large hall, with a gallery from which there is a fine view of the city below, and Nossa Senhora da Encarnação, a pilgrimage chapel up a long flight of steps. *Castle*

Towards the sea the state forest of Leiria was planted by King Diniz *State Forest*

85

to control the shifting sand dunes and is unique in that it has been maintained as a forest since its inception 600 years ago. The trees are mostly *P. pinasta* and are not tapped for resin until two years before they are due for felling. Along the sea false dunes are created to protect the areas behind them which are planted with seeds of sand-fixing plants until the soil is ready to receive the pine seedlings. All this part of Portugal is noted for its production of resin and little earthenware cups, placed below a shallow gash in the trunk of the pine to catch the precious sap, are a familiar sight.

Marinha Grande Glass Factory

Exactly half way between Leiria and the sea, Marinha Grande is noted for a glass factory which for many years made all the glass vessels in Portugal. The factory was started by an Englishman named John Beare in 1748, and 20 years later came into the possession of William Stephens and his brother John, who developed the works under the protection of the then Prime Minister, the Marques of Pombal. The brothers made an agreement that after their death the factory should be given to the State of Portugal, which was duly carried out.

Fatima

Fatima, the great pilgrimage centre, can be reached from either Batalha or Leiria. On May 13th 1917, three peasant children from the nearby village of Aljustrel, said that they saw the Blessed Virgin above a small holm oak in the Cova da Iria where they were tending their parents' sheep. The Lady told the children to return there on the 13th of each month for the next six months, which they duly did amidst great opposition from their families and the local priest. As the months went by more and more people went with the children,

Apparitions

many to pray, some to jeer. As at Lourdes, the apparition told the children to pray, especially for Russia which, as the world knows, underwent that October the Revolution which put the Communists into power. The two younger seers, a brother and sister called Francisco and Jacinta Marto, died within a few years but their cousin, Lucia dos Santos, is a Carmelite nun in Coimbra.

After a long ecclesiastical enquiry which ended in 1930, the then Bishop of Leiria, authorised public pilgrimages. Over the years more and more people from all over the world come to the shrine, particularly on May 13th and October 13th, the dates of the first and last apparitions. The enormous space – which holds a million people – in front of the new Basilica and round the tiny Chapel of the Apparitions, is usually completely filled on these days, when a Mass for the sick is celebrated on the open-air altar in front of the Basilica. There are now several hotels, and all the religious houses which have been built around the sanctuary, accept pilgrims.

Caves

Near Mira de Aire, south of Fatima a series of fantastic caves were discovered comparatively recently. Mira de Aire, with underground lakes and waterfalls, is the deepest in Europe and is served by two lifts. The other caves, Alvados and São Antonio, are very large and filled with splendid stalagmites and stalactites.

Between Fatima and Tomar, the tiny fortified village of Ourem crowns a sugarloaf hill above the town. A winding road leads up to the main gateway which is too narrow for most cars to enter but there is plenty of parking space outside. The place is fascinating, with lovely old houses surrounding the ruins of the castle, and nothing seems to have been built for at least a couple of centuries. An American couple, Mr and Mrs Joseph H. Braun, run a good restaurant, the *Adega de Cortiça*, open from April 1st to October 31st, (shut on Tuesdays). In a separate hall they give a live show of Portuguese history, with a banquet for parties of from 14 to over 100 people, but reservations for this are essential. The address is Castelos de Portugal, Ourem.

Ourem

Restaurant

A mile or two before getting into Tomar, a signpost to the right leads to the astonishing Aqueduct of Pegões. Started at the end of the 16th century to take water to the Templars Convent of Christ in Tomar, the 180 great arches stride across a remote valley, making it one of the most singular sights in the country, for no human habitation impinges on this monumental work of man.

Aqueduct of Pegões

Tomar

Tomar is one of the show cities of Portugal, for in it is the complex of the Convent of Christ, covering a hill to one side of the town, which lies on the banks of the river Nabão. Not far from the delightfully Victorian railway station, adorned with tubs of flowering plants, is the very well run tourist office which supplies a map of the town and an informative brochure in several languages. The local Tomar and Nabantino wines are especially good.

After the general suppression of the Knights Templar in 1314, the King of Portugal created the Order of Christ in 1320 to replace it, and Tomar remained as their main seat. The buildings range in age from the 12th to the 17th centuries and enclose no less than seven cloisters. The heart of this unforgettable place is the 16-arched polygon Templars' church dating from the 12th century. Entered through a splendid main doorway below a frieze of Maltese crosses, the church has a frescoed arched baldachino, reaching to the roof right round the altar. It is said that the Knights used to attend Mass on horseback, each under one of these high arches. Indeed they are just the right width for a horse and rider.

Convent of Christ

Only four of the seven cloisters are now shown, but the other three, and the long dormitory corridor upstairs, can be viewed on application to the Missionary College which is part of the same complex. The most striking and largest of the cloisters is that of the Felipes, the latest to be built. This is a brilliantly intricate two storeyed Palladian structure of 1557. Santa Barbara's Cloister, between that of the Felipes and the Hospital Cloister, is entered from the upper floor, giving the clearest view of the amazing Manueline window of the chapter house. The decoration rises from a gigantic root borne on the shoulders of an Old Man of the

Sea. The convoluted masts at either side are decorated with ropes, seaweed, marine motifs, cables and anchor chains, nets, armillary spheres and even the Order of the Garter, which was conferred on Prince Henry the Navigator who, as Grand Master, used the immense resources of the Knights to finance the voyages round Africa which he organised.

The other two cloisters shown to the public are the Cemetery Cloister and the Ablutions Cloister, where the Knights washed in the water running from Pegões.

Immaculate Conception Church

On the way down to Tomar, the purest Renaissance church in the country stands at a bend in the road. Nossa Senhora da Conceição is quite small and now completely bare, showing the perfect proportions to great advantage.

St John the Baptist Church

The parish church of St John the Baptist, in a square bounded by elegant municipal buildings, lies below the Convent of Christ. The church is unusual in having a Manueline belfry, battlemented pediment and a beautiful Gothic doorway. In the interior hang several fine primitives.

Tabuleiros Festival

Every second year the Tabuleiros Festival takes place early in July. This procession is of very ancient origin and assumed its present form in the 16th century. Young girls, dressed in white, walk in procession through the streets carrying on their heads round willow baskets on which are arranged pyramids of canes threaded through rolls of new bread and decorated with paper flowers, reaching as high as the girls bearing them and topped by a paper crown. Each girl is attended by a swain to steady the contraption. Afterwards the bread, and beef from cattle slaughtered for the purpose, are distributed to the poor.

The *Hotel dos Templários* and the *Estalagem de Santa Iria*, beautifully situated, are both four star. The *Pensão Nuno Alvares* is simple with excellent food. There are several good restaurants, some by the river.

Castelo do Bode Dam

South-east of Tomar, the lower reaches of the river Zezere have been dammed to form a large lake, the waters of which generate electricity for this part of the country. The *Pousada de São Pedro* (tel. (0049) 38159/38157), overlooks the dam and on an island in the lake, is the *Estalagem da Ilha do Lombo* with a pool. This island is further up river than the dam and is reached on a different road, going through a village called Serra.

Constancia

A road runs across the top of the dam south to Constancia, at the confluence of the Zezere and the river Tagus. The old houses of Constancia, along the river bank, are delightful. According to tradition, Camões lived here for a time and it was in this town that the British Army assembled in the Peninsular War to prepare their march into Spain for the Battle of Talavera, at which Wellington beat the French in July 1809.

Abrantes is a larger town than Constancia and lies around a castle, the ruined keep of which has been converted into a belvedere with a lovely view of the Tagus. The castle church is now an archaeological museum with later sculptures, manuscripts, vestments and local curiosities. Abrantes is the key to central Portugal and was captured by Junot in 1807, during the Peninsular War, but two years later Wellington was able to make the town his headquarters. Of the many churches in the town, the most interesting is the Renaissance Misericordia the hospital of which was founded in 1532. Fine rococo frames surround a set of lovely primitive paintings and, through the sacristy, a staircase leads to the board room of the hospital with good 18th century woodwork. The *Hotel de Turismo* is three star and there are several pensions.

Abrantes

The return to Lisbon can be made through Torres Novas – by railway or bus if you are not driving – an ancient city on the river Almonda, and grouped around a ruined 14th century castle. There are several churches including the lovely Misericordia, with an ornate ceiling painted in 1678. The church is lined with carpet *azulejos* and the altars are golden.

Torres Novas

Below Constancia the exquisite castle of Almourol, a Templars' foundation, rises on a diamond-shaped island in the middle of the Tagus. Periwinkles and many other wild flowers cover the little island. The central keep of the well-restored castle is surrounded by battlemented walls intersected by ten round towers. Strangely enough this is a castle without a history, never having been the scene of any fighting.

Almourol

South-east of Torres Novas is Golegã, scene of the biggest horse fair in the country, which takes place every year on November 10th, 11th and 12th. On these days the horse breeders of the Alentejo and the Ribatejo bring their splendid animals for sale to bullfighters and members of the international jumping team, who watch the horses parading round the ring. The *Café Restaurant Central* has good food and rooms.

*Golegã
Horse Fair*

South from Golegã, a beautiful country road goes through the flatlands by the Tagus, often on a raised causeway, owing to the winter flooding of the great river which can sometimes be glimpsed in the distance. This road comes out below the high rock on which Santarem is built, with a road winding up to the city itself.

Those interested in horse breeding and cattle raising, can cross the Tagus by a bridge, east of Golegã, and take a road down through fertile pastures on which graze herds of young cattle and horses. This is the heart of the Ribatejo, the lands on either side of the Tagus, famous for their fertility and for fine farms and stables.

The first town of general interest on this road is Alpiarça, with a

Alpiarça

89

fascinating museum, the Casa dos Patudos, which the owner, José Relvas, left to the town on his death. The museum is not open every day but application may be made locally to see it. There are tapestries and carpets and a notable collection of china and porcelain, including the exceedingly rare Chinese porcelain with European motifs, especially made for the European market. There are also Portuguese, Flemish and Italian primitives, Josefa of Obidos is represented, and there are delightful late-Victorian portraits of the José Relvas family.

Muge

Further south many important archaeological remains have been discovered at Muge, near the seat of the Dukes of Cadaval.

Vila Franca de Xira

Through the summer there are big cattle fairs at Vila Franca de Xira; the main local festival of the *Colete Encarnado* is on the first or second Sunday in July, when the bulls run through the streets accompanied by mounted *campinos*, in a beautiful costume of starched white shirts, black breeches, red cummerbunds and shining white stockings. Scarlet waistcoats partially cover the shirt and on the head is worn a green stocking cap with a red tassel on the end. While the bulls are being paraded, young men with more courage than sense, try their luck with the bulls and often have to shin up a lamppost or on to a low balcony, to save their skins.

In the town of Vila Franca, the *Estalagem da Leziria* has a good restaurant with local dishes. The *Estalagem do Gado Bravo*, over the river, also has a restaurant, and a small bullring alongside.

Santarem

The large city of Santarem is the centre of a wide region. A series of agricultural fairs take place throughout the year, the main one lasting for a fortnight at the end of May. Founded in prehistoric times, it is recorded that Julius Caesar elevated Santarem to one of the four juridical centres of Portugal when it was still called Scalabicastro.

The city, as has been mentioned already, is built on a hill above the Tagus. The town is large and retains many vestiges of its former grandeur, with flamboyant architecture, ramparts still standing and Gothic features. The shops are good and the whole place is busy and lively. There are two museums, that of Anselmo Braamcamp Ferreira, the most recent to be opened, which possesses interesting paintings, furniture and a remarkable library. In an annexe are shown a number of coaches and carriages with harnesses and other accessories, all beautifully kept.

The archaeological museum is in the secularised Romanesque-Gothic church of São João de Alporão. The Gothic tomb of Dom Duarte de Menezes was built by his wife to contain a tooth, the only thing that remained after her husband had been hacked to pieces by the Moors at Alcácer Ceguer.

The Portas do Sol, at the end of a long avenue, is enclosed by the city walls in a small public garden. From it can be seen the Tagus valley below; Palgrave, who edited 'The Golden Treasury', came here with Tennyson in 1859 and considered this view to be 'one of the great panoramic landscapes of Europe'.

Portas do Sol

The city is filled with churches, of which the most striking façade belongs to the Seminary in the Praça Sá da Bandeira, not unlike that of a grand royal palace. The Marvila church is extremely lofty and the three aisles are covered with diamond-patterned *azulejos* entirely covering the interior and increasing in size until they reach the plain, coffered roof. The whole austere building, which is believed to have been started by the Templars in the 12th century, is very satisfying in its noble proportions. The *Hotel Abidis* is two star and there are many restaurants.

South of the road which goes straight across country from Santarem to Caldas da Rainha through Rio Maior, where there are opencast natural mineral salt deposits, the region down to Lisbon is exceedingly beautiful. The Serra de Montejunto strides across the northern part, descending into highly cultivated, fertile vineyards and fields of maize. South of the Serra, the motorway north from Lisbon by-passes the ancient city of Alenquer. Special mention should be made of Meca, near Alenquer, a small 18th century village leading up to an avenue of tall white poplar trees in front of the formal, late 18th century church. This is dedicated to Santa Quiteira who protects the unwary against mad dogs, fortunately still unknown in Portugal.

Meca

Among other lovely towns, or large villages, in this part of the country is Merciana, which contains the best late-Renaissance building near Lisbon. This is the church of Nossa Senhora da Piedade with an exquisite chancel arch, dated 1535. Nearby, at Aldeia Galega de Merciana, there is another three-aisled church with beautiful columns and a painted ceiling. In the same village is the unspoilt church of Nossa Senhora dos Prazeres, all white and gold, with cherubs and female caryatids supporting the ambones.

Merciana

Aldeia Galega de Merciana

South of Runa, where there is a home for retired regular officers and a small museum of interesting canvases, the soil turns red near Pero Negro, and is very fertile. Dois Portos, Sapateria and São Quintinho are all worth seeing by those interested in ecclesiastical architecture of various periods. The first named, has a church with a most unusual wooden ceiling carved in a carpet pattern, Sapateria one with notable early patterned tiles, and that in São Quintinho is lined, like the church in Moncarapacho, with early Persian carpet-like tiled rectangles each with a different pattern reaching up to the ceiling of the three-aisled 16th century building.

Historians will discover redoubts and fortifications pertaining to the Lines of Torres Vedras on all the hills in this beautiful and fertile part of the country.

Guarda Cathedral

The Mountains

Beira Baixa and Beira Alta

North-west of Lisbon and the Tagus are the central mountains of the country, culminating in the heights of the Serra da Estrela which stretches right across from the Serra da Lousã, below Coimbra, to Guarda on the way to Spain. The first town of importance in this wide stretch of country going up to the Spanish frontier, is Castelo Branco, the capital of Beira Baixa or Lower Beira.

Castelo Branco

The city is large and prosperous and is grouped around a big public garden, with a tourist office in it. The chief curiosity of the city is the garden of the former episcopal palace, next to the museum. The garden, though on a small scale, is filled with stone pools and decorated with emblems such as dolphins and pillars surmounted by crowns. Statues of Portuguese kings border formal steps, while those of the Spanish kings, Philip I and Philip II, under whom the country suffered the occupation from 1580 to 1640, are half the size of the kings of Portugal. Another staircase has statues of saints at either side, each identified for the curious. The topiary work which

Bishop's Palace Gardens

92

encloses all the flower beds, gives a delicious scent and the whole place is a singular example of garden planning.

The museum in the episcopal palace is arranged in lovely rooms which set off the comparatively few exhibits. There are some good primitives and a series of portraits of former bishops – the diocese is now joined to that of Portalegre – which vary very much in quality. The intelligent face of Dom João de Mendonça, who designed the garden, stands out from his colleagues. Good English prints of the Peninsular War period and delightful beach scenes by Costa Camelo adorn the walls of many of the rooms. A touching exhibit is the slate tombstone of Thomas Stewart Armiger, who died on August 19th, 1810, aged only 20. He must have lost his life in one of the many skirmishes which took place around here during the Peninsular War.

Museum

English Prints

At one end of the museum the embroidery school keeps alive the great tradition of Castelo Branco embroideries; some of the early bedspreads are on show in the museum. Embroideries can be ordered and there is a large selection of patterns from which to choose. They are usually worked in somewhat muted colours on fine linen.

Embroidery

The city is strangely lacking in hotels. The pensions are adequate, the restaurants dull.

Below Castelo Branco, and towering over the Tagus, is the elegant rectangular castle of Belver, which belonged to the Order of Hospitalers of St John of Jerusalem and was rebuilt by Nuno Alvares Pereira, the Holy Constable of Portugal, in 1390. The small town of whitewashed houses is delightful.

Belver

North-east of Castelo Branco there are several places to visit. Idanha-a-Nova, near a great dam, possesses the ruins of a Templars' castle. Surrounded by ancient houses, the 18th century *solar*, or manor house, of the Marques de Graciosa is of interest. On the first week-end in April, the small shrine of Nossa Senhora de Almortão, at the end of a by-road, is the scene of one of the biggest *romarias*, or pilgrimages, in this part of the country. It is an unforgettable experience to mingle with the crowd of country men, women and children who sing and suddenly break into dance, to the strange sounds of the *adufe*, a square tambourine. As always at these *romarias*, there is a fair with local products for sale – including pottery, locally woven materials and handicrafts – and a Mass is said in the small chapel, in which are hung attractively primitive *ex voto* pictures.

Idanha-a-Nova

Fair

East of Idanha-a-Nova there is a frontier post at Segura, once completely walled, but with little left now of the original fortifications, except for a large gateway and a Roman bridge. The town is very picturesque with a fine Manueline *pelourinho*, or village cross, and a Manueline Misericordia church. It was through here

Segura

that the first contingent of Napoleonic troops, under Junot, entered Portugal in November 1807, at the beginning of the Peninsular War.

Idanha-a-Velha

North from Idanha-a-Nova, Idanha-a-Velha is a small place, all that remains of a flourishing Roman city situated on a Celtic settlement. It was an episcopal city until 1199 when the See was moved to Guarda. The church, a Paleo-Christian basilica, is of an immense age and is believed to have been built on an even earlier Visgothic place of worship. There are dozens of Roman inscriptions preserved within the church and, in the chapel of São Damaso, there are Roman coins and pottery on show.

Monsanto

This strange village, looking almost Iron Age in its primitiveness, was once voted to be the most Portuguese village in Portugal. A complete misnomer, as it is not in any way a typical Portuguese village, which, as we have seen, is usually clean and whitewashed, though in the northern parts, there are many houses and cottages built of natural, undressed stone. Monsanto, with practically no viable road inside the village, is built up against a steep hill, crowned by a square-built fortress. The small, solid houses are inserted between huge, round granite boulders so that at a distance the whole place melts into the rugged landscape. The local people are exceptionally well built and handsome, though few of the women now wear their original costume of stiff, black hooded capes over white linen shirts.

Each year, on May 3rd, the historical procession of the Marafonas takes place, when the young girls of the village throw baskets of flowers from the ramparts in commemoration of the legend that, when the castle was besieged for a long time, those inside threw down a calf to convince their enemies that they still had plenty of food.

Monfortinho Spa

The famous Spa of Monfortinho beyond Monsanto, is very near the Spanish frontier. The waters alleviate, and often cure, diseases of the liver and kidneys, as well as skin trouble. There are several excellent hotels grouped around the elegant thermal centre, of which the best known is the *Fonte Santa*. Its restaurant is noted.

Gois

An extremely twisting road, some 90 miles in length, goes from Castelo Branco over a series of low mountain ranges to Coimbra. This road, with splendid views, passes through scattered villages, but the first place of interest is Gois, built up like a pyramid. There is a Manueline bridge and a beautiful town hall with 17th century allegorical paintings on the ceilings. In the parish church is a superb Renaissance tomb, by Diogo Torralva, showing a kneeling knight set in a carved surround, and there are 16th century panels on the high altar.

Serra da Lousã

Many of the villages in these hills have become deserted in the last few years owing to the flight to the towns and widespread emigra-

94

tion to France and Germany. When emigrants go from the Minho and Tras-os-Montes and the upper Beira, they always return with money they have saved to rebuild their houses and buy more land. Unhappily, those from the Serra da Lousã, do not seem to have such close ties with their native villages, though most of these have electricity, street lighting and piped water. Perhaps when the movement of the return to the land reaches Portugal, these often delightful villages, with beautiful views, will once again be brought to life.

North of Castelo Branco on the way to Covilhã, Alpedrinha is an extremely early settlement, believed to have been founded before the Roman occupation. There are splendid old houses in the village and a huge 18th century monumental fountain at one side of a large and elegant ruined house, the unglazed 18th century windows of which give on to the roofless remains within. The *Estalagem S. Jorge* is four star, perfect for a rest cure.

Alpedrinha

Castelo Novo is another delightful place at the end of a short road, off to the left before Alpedrinha, in the foothills of the Serra da Guardunha. The council chamber, fronted by a Manueline village cross, is very early and the great house of the Falcãos is a typical early 17th century house. On the edge of the village, a strange, shell-like depression carved out of the granite rock was used in bygone times for the treading of grapes. This part of the country is particularly rich in bird life. Eagles hover overhead and it is a resting place for storks in the spring.

Castelo Novo

Birds

Covilhã is situated in that part of the country known as the Cova da Beira and is an excursion centre for the mountains of the Serra da Estrela and for the only winter sports resort in the country, Penhas da Saude. The town is a great wool centre and the local mills turn out most of the yarn for the country's woollen industry. The flocks of sheep which graze over the wide, fertile uplands of the Cova da Beira, also supply the milk from which the delicious Serra cheese (*queijo da Serra*) is made. From Covilhã roads lead over the wild mountains to Seia and, via Manteigas, to Gouveia. On a hill, above Manteigas, is the *Pousada de São Lourenço* (tel. (0059) 47150), with magnificent views. Covilhã contains several pensions and the four star *Estalagem da Varanda das Carqueijais*.

Covilhã

North-east of Covilhã, Belmonte is a fascinating town, with a castle rising from slabs of granite. The town was the birthplace of Pedro Alvares Cabral who discovered Brazil in 1500. He was baptized in the small, Romanesque parish church which contains an interesting, granite, Gothic group of the Descent from the Cross. Off the church, in a Renaissance chapel, are the tombs of the Cabral family.

Belmonte

A mile north of Belmonte is the strange Roman edifice of Centum Cellas. A square, granite building of three floors it has not been over-restored, fortunately. Its original use has never been disco-

Centum Cellas

vered; it could have been a small temple, a military outpost or even a prison, though this is unlikely as the walls are interspersed with large windows.

Penamacor

North of Monsanto, Penamacor stands high over endless arable land with only a few cork oaks and olives in the more sheltered spots. Within the outer walls of the very large castle, there is a village of low, dark houses built of granite blocks. The lower part of the town is also medieval, many of the houses having Manueline windows, as does the old city hall, built above the arched entrance to the town.

Sortelha

The fortified village of Sortelha, east of Belmonte, is on the way to Sabugal. It is a most curious sight, with huge 12th century walls surrounding the village, which like so many other places is this part of the country, is built straight onto granite outcrops. A kind of platform above the entrance to the high castle keep could be used for throwing down boiling oil on assailants. Outside the main entrance to the castle, is a most elegant 16th century *pelourinho*.

Sabugal

A 13th century bridge crosses the river Coa at the entrance to Sabugal, a country town which is also dominated by a castle. The five-sided keep, built in 1297, is most unusual.

Guarda

The capital of Beira Alta, or Upper Beira, Guarda is the highest town in Portugal, some 3,500 ft above sea level. Built on the eastern slopes of the Serra da Estrela, it is on the direct route, both by rail and road, to Madrid and the northern part of Spain, the frontier post being at Vilar Formoso. Many of the streets have arcaded houses. The four star *Hotel de Turismo* is one of the few really good hotels in this part of the country, so Guarda is an excellent centre for exploring the many towns of interest within a radius of 50 miles. Guarda itself cannot be described as lively in terms of entertainment – or restaurants – for the visitor.

Accommoda-
tion

Cathedral

The cathedral, or Sé, is strangely French in feeling. Begun in 1390 and made of blocks of solid granite, it was completed only in the 16th century, with twisted Manueline pillars to the chancel arch. The nave leads up to a great altar piece with a hundred figures carved, it is believed, by the Frenchman, Jean de Rouen, who did so much work around Coimbra. The choir stalls are unusual, as a different face is carved under the seat of each one, many looking as if they might have been done from live models. *Son et Lumière* is sometimes staged here in July and August.

Son et
Lumière

Museum

The regional museum is in the former diocesan seminary and apart from archaeological exhibits and Portuguese primitive paintings, there is a collection of weights and measures from the time of King Manuel I in the late 15th century.

The solid Torre dos Ferreiros is another feature of this ancient

Fishermen's beach, Cascais

Silves

Albufeira

Algarve farmer

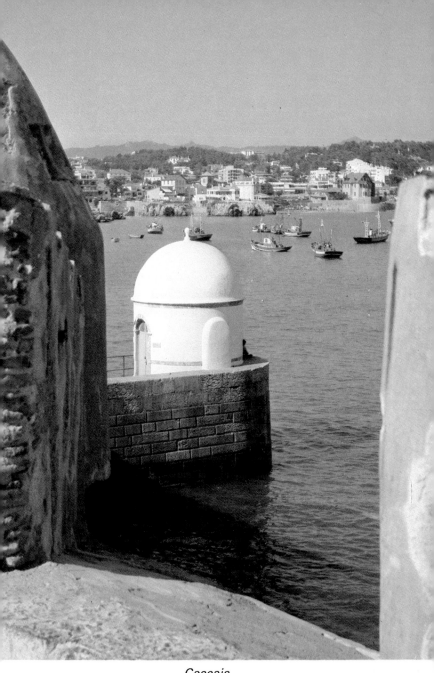

Cascais

Bullfight

Roman temple at Evora

town, as are the two gateways which remain of the old fortifications.

North-east of Guarda, through lovely remote country, the city of Pinhel was once an Episcopal See and the centre, like many of these border towns, of much fighting over the years; there are the remains of a castle with a couple of high towers. Among the fine houses of the little city, is the former episcopal palace, built at the end of the 18th century and the city hall of the same period. The latter has a small archaeological museum, with a few later exhibits. Just before reaching Pinhel from Guarda, there is a large dolmen, the Anta da Pêra do Moço, a huge block of granite on five supporting stones. The region is famous for its wine.

Pinhel

The parish church of Figueira de Castelo Rodrigo possesses a possibly unique arch supporting the choir, constructed entirely of S-shaped stones fitting into one another without any key stone. Its belfry has been the nesting place of storks for hundreds of years.

Figueira de Castelo Rodrigo

The Pensions, *Central* and *Santos* with restaurants, are both two star.

Almeida, which can be reached only by a road south of Figueira de Castelo Rodrigo to Vilar Formoso, is one of the most unusual towns in Portugal. The houses are all contained within the huge star-shaped fortifications which Vaubon completed in the 18th century. The 12 salients differ in size, but in each of them the granite walls rise from a 40 ft deep ditch which would be a moat in more northern lands. These salients and lookout posts are distinct from the town itself which lies within an inner series of fortifications. It is possible to walk round the top of the walls, thus seeing the layout of a fortress which was of primary importance from the time of the first king of Portugal down to the Peninsular War, during which both Wellington and Massena took the citadel in turns. The only access to the town is along three tunnel-like entrances through the great walls, approached by bridges spanning the ditch.

Almeida

North-west of Guarda, and just north of the Serra da Estrela, Celorico da Beira is a typical Beira town. The castle is square, the walls enclosing a battlemented tower. The parish church was turned into a hospital for the British army during the final phases of the Peninsular War. It possesses some fine paintings and a beautiful painted, coffered ceiling.

Celorico da Beira

Two two star pensions are the *Mondego* and the *Parque* and there is a café restaurant, the *Tobé*.

The road north from Celorico, passes near Trancoso, a completely walled city with arcaded streets and many fine houses. In the large space where the Fair of St Bartolomeu is held in August, stands a six-sided granite and whitewashed chapel dedicated to the Saint.

Trancoso

Fair

Also outside the city walls, is the Fonte Nova, or new fountain. Built in 1589, it resembles a small Greek temple.

The wide stretch of country west of Trancoso, bounded by the Douro on the north, by the Viseu-Guarda road on the south and that from Lamego to Viseu on the east, is roughly a hundred miles square and is filled with interesting and little-known places. It is crossed by one main road through exceptionally lovely country. The almond trees here flower in early March, much later than those in the Algarve.

Penedono   Between this road and the Douro, is the tiny heart-shaped battlemented castle of Penedono. Below the clustered rocks from which the castle springs, stands an elegant *pelourinho* and a small church with fine Baroque details. In the Lusiads, Camões, the Portuguese epic poet, relates that the Knight of Penedono was one of the 12 Knights of Portugal who, legend relates, were asked by John of Gaunt's son-in-law, King Diniz of Portugal, to go to England to joust for the honour of 12 English ladies. It is these Knights who are depicted in the iridescent tiled panels in the gardens of the Palace of Fronteira, at São Domingos de Benfica near Lisbon.

Marialva   Some 15 miles north of Trancoso, the town of Marialva lies off the road to the left. The modern village, with blinding whitewashed walls, lies below the grey ruins of the castle, within which the little houses of the original settlement are deserted and falling into ruin, as is the chapel. The 15th century *pelourinho* is notable.

Lamego

On one of the main roads south of Tras-os-Montes over the Douro, Lamego is set in the midst of great orchards and vineyards. It is an almost completely Baroque town with few modern additions in the centre. Set around the main square are noble buildings with granite pediments, doorways and window surrounds, standing out from whitewashed façades.

The four star *Estalagem de Lamego* has few rooms, the one star *Hotel Parque*, many more. The pensions in the town are pleasant and the local food delicious – smoked raw hams are eaten with melon or figs in season, and *paio*, smoked loin of pork, is good.

Museum   The Bishop's Palace is now a museum with some unforgettable exhibits, including an extraordinary panel of the 'Creation of the Wild Beasts by the Eternal Father'. This is one of five panels by Grão Vasco from the Cathedral. There are also some particularly splendid 16th century Flemish tapestries, early polychrome sculptures and whole chapels from the Chagas Convent which was pulled down at the beginning of this century, though the church remains, with a monumental painted ceiling and golden retables.

Cathedral   Also in the main square is the cathedral, or Sé. Originally

98

Romanesque, there are additions from almost every period since then. The double cloister at the side is elegant and simple, with the marble tomb of the founder, Bishop Noronha, in a small Gothic chapel lined with 18th century *azulejos* depicting the life of St Nicholas. All the other churches of this country town contain notable Baroque features, and one of the most remarkable examples of this style in Portugal, is the great pilgrimage shrine of Nossa Senhora dos Remédios, on the summit of a wooded hill, dominating the town.

The large church is approached by a huge granite and whitewashed double staircase, with nine landings, leading up to a circular courtyard in front of the church. This courtyard is surrounded by obelisks, arches and high granite pillars, many crowned with superbly carved figures of heroic size, some in oriental garments, some in classical draperies. Balustrades, ornamented with spheres and vases, surround the landings and stairways and elegant fountains with water trickling out of masked faces and dolphins' heads, are on the terraces. A big pilgrimage and fair takes place around this church every year at the beginning of September, and is well worth seeing.

Nossa Senhora dos Remédios

A few miles south of Lamego, there are the remains of a famous Cistercian monastery at São João de Tarouca. The church, with beautiful choir stalls and Baroque altars, is mainly visited for its primitive canvases including a great picture of St Peter seated on a throne, of which the authorship has been much disputed. It is now attributed to Cristóvão de Figueiredo and is believed to be the original of the very similar picture in the gallery at Viseu.

São João de Tarouca

Not far from Tarouca, in the small village of Ucanha, a fortified bridge passes over the river Varosa under a massive 15th century tower.

Ucanha

Near Ucanha, in the village of Salzedas, is another Cistercian monastery of which the greater part is still standing. The church, one of the largest in Portugal, was consecrated in 1225 but the whole place was completely remodelled in the 18th century.

Salzedas

Further south, towards Trancoso, a turning to the right leads to the extremely interesting town of Aguiar da Beira, built entirely of granite. Behind the central square, from which rises a most graceful *pelourinho*, a small, square keep adjoins what must be the medieval council chamber, with a stone bench running round the walls. The town spring is below this unusual building, entered by a Gothic doorway. There are also the remains of a drystone fortress, which might well be Iron Age. Aguiar da Beira is so remote and primitive, that visitors on the lookout for a really remarkable example of a small medieval town should make the effort to visit it.

Aguiar da Beira

The road due south from Lamego to Viseu goes through wonderful high, wild uplands with mountains on either side, and near the

Castro Daire	road there are many Neolithic remains. Castro Daire, the only place of any size on this 40 mile stretch of lonely road, is set on a high bluff and the road winds up and through it. Lovely houses surround the main square, and the whole place has a beautiful, secluded charm.
São Pedro do Sul	To the south of Castro Daire, a road to the right leads to São Pedro do Sul, with good hotels at the *Termas*, or Spa, three kilometres away. The town possesses many fine buildings. The town hall occupies a magnificent Baroque friary. The church is filled with rich ornamentation of golden retables, fine statues, silver sanctuary lamps and a lovely organ dated 1729, while a beautiful ceiling and fittings distinguish the sacristy. The façade of the Misericordia is entirely covered with pale blue and white tiles, set among convoluted granite windows. This is near the fascinating balconied façade of the Reriz palace.
Caramulo	A road from São Pedro do Sul through Vouzela leads to Caramulo, and there is another way, through Viseu. Caramulo has an excellent *pousada*, that of *São Jerónimo* (tel. (0032) 86291). The place is noted for the remarkable museum which was founded by the Fundação Abel Laçerda. The paintings include not only Portuguese and other primitives, but also 17th, 18th and 19th century work, culminating in a collection of contemporary painting. This includes a superb wash drawing by Salvador Dali of a naked man, brandishing a shield, on a prancing grey Lusitanian horse. The painter gave it to this museum in 1954, and Picasso presented a typical still life.

In addition to paintings, the collection contains bronzes, Chinese porcelain, sculpture, silver, furniture, tapestries and carpets. There is also a department devoted to vintage cars.

Viseu

A rival to Lamego in being one of the most lovely towns in this part of the country, Viseu is filled with Baroque houses, and the cathedral square is one of the finest in Portugal. It is in the centre of the old town, to which entrance is through a 15th century arched gateway. At one side stands the solid, almost fortified cathedral, the two low towers enclosing a Renaissance façade. To the side is the museum, in the former episcopal palace, and exactly opposite, across the great space, in the centre of which stands an elegant *pelourinho*, is the wide and beautiful twin-towered 18th century façade of the Misericordia church.

Cathedral	The cathedral, originally Romanesque, has a strange vaulted Manueline roof with knotted cables supported on the 13th century columns clustered along the nave. The golden retable of the high altar is 17th century and above, is a superbly painted ceiling in many colours. The sacristy ceiling is painted in freer style, and depicts satyrs, wild boars and monkeys with tropical flowers and

foliage. Round the walls are beautiful vestment chests, and blue and yellow carpet tiles.

The cathedral possesses a rich treasury, which is displayed in the chapter house, off the cloister. In addition to church vessels, there are Limoges enamels, vestments and polychrome statues.

The Viseu school of painting was flourishing in the 16th century. It was led by Gaspar Vaz and Vasco Fernandes under strong Flemish influence. Grão Vasco's altarpieces in the Lamego museum and in the parish church at Freixo de Espada à Cinta, as well as his many works in this museum, show great originality and tenderness. The realism of his backgrounds is inspired by local subjects. Paintings on view range from these primitives to a large collection of the works of Columbano Bordalo Pinheiro, the most remarkable Portuguese painter of the late 19th century. There are also a number of sculptures ranging in date from the 13th to the 18th centuries.

Grão Vasco Museum

The town is a centre for fine cabinet making as well as for antiques, though not all are genuine. Several of the churches, particularly those of the Carmo, São Francisco and São Bento possess good early canvases, often set in beautiful Baroque frames.

The Almeida Moreira museum is in the house of its namesake, the first Director of the Grão Vasco museum in 1915, who left his residence, and its contents, to the city. It is a charming collection of antique furniture, old tiles, ceramics and Portuguese paintings of the end of the last century and the beginning of this. The library is also open to the public.

Almeida Moreira Museum

The best hotel is the four star *Grão Vasco* and there are many pensions. Restaurants include *Alvorada*, Rua Gaspar Barreiros 24, *Capucha*, Praça da Republica 16 and *Gruta*, Rua D. Duarte 25. *Chanfana*, lamb stewed in red wine, is a local speciality.

East of Viseu, the road to Celorico da Beira goes through Mangualde, in the centre of which is the lovely Palacio Anadia. The old hospital, at the side of the little 18th century Misericordia, is also delightful.

Mangualde

Seven miles up the Aguiar da Beira road from Mangualde, at Penalva do Castelo, is another splendid country house, the Casa da Insua; it cannot be seen from the road, but visitors are often allowed to go into the gardens and the courtyard.

Penalva do Castelo

South-west of Mangualde, at Canas de Senhorim, is the excellent three star *Hotel de Urgeiriça* (tel. 67267). Set in deep country, with vineyards and woodlands, the hotel is extremely comfortable, and the public rooms are not unlike those in an old fashioned country house, with huge fires and great vases of brilliant flowers. There is a swimming pool and tennis courts, and a number of individual chalets in the grounds.

Canas de Senhorim

South of Canas de Senhorim and of the Mondego, lies the main road from Coimbra to Guarda. Beautiful but winding, with the great mass of the Serra da Estrela to the right, it passes near many fascinating places.

Lourosa
Lourosa has a church dating from pre-Romanesque times. There are remarkable early iron grilles in the interior and visitors can see that the whole unusual edifice is constructed of stone from older Visigothic and Moorish buildings, thus making it one of the most primitive places of worship in the country. The Manueline *pelourinho* nearby, should also be noted.

Avô
A very short way along the main highway, an extremely twisting road to the right, with lovely views, leads, in a couple of miles, to the tiny, castellated village of Avô, jutting out into the narrow river Alva. The castle has been rebuilt, but even so the place is so unusual, that it is worth the detour to see it. Perched above the water, the houses are mostly built of granite, though some are relieved by whitewashed walls, as is the parish church.

Oliveira do Hospital
Back to the highway, Oliveira do Hospital is set in vineclad country. The parish church is notable for the superb ceiling painted in perspective and for the very early tombs, with reclining figures carved in Ança stone.

There is a pension and the two star *Hotel São Paulo*.

Seia
The Pousada de Santa Barbara (tel. (0037) 52252), is at Póvoa das Quartas, further along the main road. Then comes Seia, a mile along a side road to the right, from where begin two of the roads over the Serra da Estrela.

Nossa Senhora do Espinheiro
Near Seia is the Gothic pilgrimage chapel of Nossa Senhora do Espinheiro (thorn bush), where a big *romaria* attracting all the people and shepherds round about takes place in September, when the statue of the Holy Child, dressed in a Captain's uniform, with a top hat and riding boots, is taken in procession out of the chapel.

Gouveia is the starting point for a road across the Estrela mountains to Manteigas, already mentioned. Several lakes and waterfalls in these mountains reward the walker with their lonely beauty.

Linhares
Standing high in the foothills of the Estrela mountains, towards Celorico da Beira, Linhares is at the end of a winding road. The village is filled with large country houses, some of which are almost in ruins. The castle has two high towers; the town hall and an unusual council chamber are beside it. Apart from the fact that every building in the place is either beautiful or interesting, both the parish church and the Misericordia are filled with remarkable Portuguese primitive paintings. To find such riches in so remote a spot is astonishing.

Aveiro

Coimbra and the Gold Coast

Coimbra

Coimbra, capital of the Beira Litoral province, is one of the most fascinating cities in Portugal, formed around the University which was founded in 1290, at about the same time that the Schools in Oxford and Cambridge assumed similar status. The city is built on a hill, going down to the river Mondego, wide in the winter rains, a mere trickle of water between sandbanks in the summer. Rising north of Guarda, the Mondego is the only one of Portugal's great rivers, the Tagus, the Mondego and the Douro, to rise in Portugal; the other two have their sources in Spain, that of the Tagus is beyond Madrid.

Beira Litoral

The main buildings of the University are grouped around a large courtyard from one side of which an 18th century tower dominates the city. The Sala dos Capelos, or University Hall, has a good 17th century painted ceiling. The most important building in the University is the great early 18th century Library, Biblioteca, which, with that of Mafra, gives Portugal two of the most beautiful libraries in the world. It is entered by a noble portal, surmounted by the coat of arms of King John V who built the Library between 1717 and 1728. The three great rooms of which it consists are almost

University

Library

perfect cubes, each with galleries supported on unusual tall inverted pyramids, richly gilded. In each room the gilding is allied to different and most subtle colours – a deep green, a paler green and a wonderful Chinese lacquer red. The monumental arches rising to almost the full height of the rooms lead up to a contemporary portrait of King John V set in a looped, curtain-like frame. This lovely building is still used by the fortunate undergraduates.

University
Chapel
The University chapel is an extraordinary mixture of Manueline and 17th and 18th century styles. The Baroque organ and the repainted barrel ceiling are particularly fine, as are the 17th century patterned *azulejos* on the walls. The silver sanctuary lamp, and the chancel arch, outlined in gold, are Manueline.

The Students
The students wear long black capes, ragged at the hem with every tear, it is said, marking an amorous adventure. There is a great tradition of *fado* singing, different from the Lisbon *fado* in intellectual and sentimental content. Many of the undergraduates live, and have done for hundreds of years, in what are called *republicas*, consisting of about a dozen students from the same region, who live communally in rented lodgings, sharing expenses. The academic year ends in May with the Queima das Fitas, when the students burn their Faculty ribbons – red for Law, yellow for Medicine, a Faculty which dates from the 14th century, and blue for Letters.

Machado
de Castro
Museum
The Machado de Castro museum is in the former episcopal palace near the University. It contains the best collection of early polychrome stone statues in the country, for Coimbra was the centre of a great school of sculpture. Particularly notable is the series of Apostles in life size painted terracotta, by the Frenchman Philippe Houdart, who worked in Coimbra in the early 1550s. There are also some beautiful early-Portuguese paintings including one of the Assumption of the Blessed Virgin by the Master of Sardoal, who takes his name from the village near Abrantes.

The church plate, with a 12th century silver gilt chalice, is notable and lovely vestments include delightfully gaudy 18th century chasubles from Macau.

Old Cathedral
The heart of Coimbra is not large and the most interesting buildings are mainly around the University. The old cathedral, Sé Velha, surmounted by battlements, has been drastically restored back to its original Romanesque appearance. Saint Anthony of Padua, born in Lisbon, was ordained priest in this cathedral.

University
Press
The first university press was set up in the cloisters adjoining this cathedral, and functioned there until the beginning of this century. The cathedral square is surrounded by old houses and narrow one-way streets go down to the river. Incidentally, Coimbra is not a difficult city in which to park.

The new cathedral, Sé Nova, is a late 17th century building transitional between Renaissance and Baroque styles. The golden high altar and many canvases and statues, are all enclosed in beautiful altarpieces and the whole great space is much enlivened by jolly Baroque angels of all sizes, some even flying around the lantern of the cupola, while others with Prince of Wales feathers on their little heads, blow trumpets.

New Cathedral

Nearer the river is the famous Augustinian monastery of Santa Cruz. A Baroque porch stands, strangely detached, from the Manueline façade. The church is long and narrow and contains splendid carvings, in particular those of the Renaissance pulpit and, on either side of the chancel, the tombs of King Afonso Henriques and King Manuel I. The 17th century sacristy, with fine canvases, including one of Pentecost attributed to Grão Vasco, should be seen, as should the lovely Cloister of Silence, of two storeys and in strangely uncluttered Manueline. Off this cloister is a staircase to the upper choir with early 16th century choir stalls, the pinky-red and gold backs of which are surmounted by golden high relief carvings of the voyages of Vasco da Gama. These are dated 1505 and are the finest of their type in the country.

Santa Cruz Monastery

Santo Antonio dos Olivais, in the suburbs of the city to the northeast, is an 18th century group of buildings on the site of the 13th century friary in which St Anthony of Padua became a Franciscan. A three-arched entrance, under a pediment, leads to a flight of steps at the sides of which are small chapels containing 18th century terracotta groups of the life of Christ. The church itself is small, with early blue and white tiled panels of the life of St Anthony. But it is the sacristy which is of particular interest. The 18th century vestment chests and tiled pictures are set below charming canvases of the life of the saint, enclosed in golden panels of the richest Baroque woodwork. The *romaria*, on Whit Monday, is held in the space all around the church, enclosed by low houses.

Santo Antonio dos Olivais

Coimbra is fortunate in having very fine public parks, of which the most splendid is the park, or *Mata*, of Santa Cruz. It is laid out with monumental staircases, statues, tile-backed benches and a famous 18th century waterfall.

Santa Cruz Park

The Botanical Gardens, nearer the river, also have fine architectural features and a splendid collection of trees, flowers and shrubs.

Botanical Gardens

Over the bridge, on the south side of the river, stands the ruined Santa Clara a Velha where the body of Inez de Castro lay before it was transferred to Alcobaça. The Rua Antonio Augusto Gonçalves at the side, leads to the House of Tears, Quinta das Lágrimas, a private house where visitors are allowed in to the gardens and can see the spring bubbling up over red stones, which it is said were first observed after the murder of Inez de Castro at this place, hence its name.

House of Tears

Children's Village

Back on the main road from the bridge is the entrance to the Children's Village, or Portugal dos Pequeninos. This is a small park in which are models of many different types of Portuguese houses and the principal monuments of the country – a delight for young children and even of interest to their elders.

Santa Clara à Nova Convent

The great pile of the convent and church of Santa Clara à Nova, stands on a hill nearby. The church is impressive with a coffered stone roof and Doric pilasters. St Elizabeth of Portugal founded the original Poor Clare convent when she was a widow, and round the chancel are six enchanting early 18th century canvases of the translation of the relics of the Holy Queen, from the original Gothic tomb in the lower choir to a silver shrine, which still stands on the high altar. The saint's figure, dressed as a Poor Clare nun, lies on top of this original 14th century tomb with her two dogs beside her. Polychromed stone figures of the nuns, each different, stand around one side and the Apostles on the other, and the sarcophagus is supported on the backs of resting lions.

Cloister

Carlos Mardel, the military architect who designed many of the fountains all over Lisbon, built the classical cloister in the middle of the 18th century. It is large and satisfying in the sobriety of its proportions. The upper choir of the church should also be seen. There is a small museum of ecclesiastical art, agreeable early frescoes on the backs of the choir stalls and good polychrome statues.

Accommodation

There is no luxury hotel in Coimbra; the oldest and best known is the three star *Astoria*, by the bridge over the river and near the tourist office. Other hotels are the three star *Oslo* and *Braganca*, one star *Mondego* and *Avenida* and several pensions. The *Restaurant Santa Cruz*, at the side of the church of the same name, has good food. Incidentally, the local Bussaco wine is particularly good. As it does not travel well it is almost impossible to find away from this region. Cafés abound in which to sit and sample Bussaco, and, as in every other part of Portugal, they stay open late and provide pleasant vantage points from which to experience local life.

Rice Fields

Down the river Mondego are some of the biggest rice growing properties in the country. In former times, teams of oxen drew special ploughs over the watery paddies to prepare the ground for the sowing in May. Now paddies are ploughed by special tractors, with enormous wheels, the ploughman sitting high above the waters, and sowing is done from low-flying aeroplanes.

Montemor-o-Velho

On the north bank of the river stands the medieval castle of Montemor-o-Velho, crowning a hill above the town. Built on the site of a Roman military outpost, the present fortress is fundamentally 14th century in date. A good road leads right in to the great courtyard surrounded by battlemented walls, from which a marvellous view of the lower reaches of the Mondego can be seen

A large watering place at the mouth of the Mondego, which is here crossed by a bridge, Figueira da Foz is particularly popular with tourists. The huge, sandy beach lies for two miles along a wide curve, but being exposed to the full force of the Atlantic, is not always safe for bathing. The town is large and cheerful with a most unusual collection of 18th century Dutch glazed tiles in the Casa do Paço, now the Chamber of Commerce, each portraying a different scene.

Figueira da Foz

The local museum contains a variety of objects, including archaeological remains, with a notable gold disc dating from the 3rd century BC. There are also coins and medals, arms, textiles, ceramics and porcelain, carpets, furniture, paintings and even collections of fans and walking sticks, altogether a fascinating conglomeration.

Museum

Figueira da Foz has many good hotels and pensions. The tourist office on the ocean front has particulars of these and of local restaurants. There is a casino, with a theatre where concerts are held, as well as gambling rooms.

Accommodation

Casino

The road from Coimbra along the north bank of the Mondego to Figueira da Foz, passes Tentugal with several interesting churches. The parish church has a large painted stone reredos to the high altar with similarly decorated side chapels, one with a very early wrought iron gate. These stone reredoses and finely carved tombs, many with recumbent and kneeling figures, are a feature of this part of the country. They are made of *pedra de ançã*, the soft, honey-coloured local stone which hardly discolours with time.

Tentugal

The church in the tiny village of São Marcos, on a side road between Tentugal and Coimbra, contains some of the most remarkable Renaissance tombs in Portugal as well as early Gothic ones, and the famous chapel of the Reis Magos, or Three Kings. The high altar reredos is by Nicolas Chanterene, the sculptor of so much fine work around Coimbra.

São Marcos

On the main road south from Coimbra, the village of Condeixa-a-Nova, now by-passed, contains superb 18th century houses along the main street. A mile to the south-east, and well signposted, are the widespread Roman remains of Conimbriga, the largest to have been excavated in the country.

Condeixa-a-Nova

Conimbriga

The Romans started building here on a pre-Celtic site. Oddly enough, it is known that Conimbriga was the seat of a bishopric when Christianity first penetrated the Iberian peninsula and only in the 9th century, when Conimbriga was already in ruins, did the bishop move to Coimbra, which by then, having taken its name from Conimbriga, had greatly increased in importance.

The ruins include several houses, of which the layouts can be clearly seen, and a great variety of mosaic floors, not only patterned but also representing dolphins, birds, fish, faces, and a man leading a donkey with a figure astride it. These mosaics have recently been treated in such a way that they are protected from the weather and so can be seen in their entirety. There is a small museum and a good café attached to it.

Semide

A few miles south of Coimbra on the way to Mirando do Corvo, the 17th century Benedictine monastery at Semide has two cloisters; the church has a fine organ, good choir stalls and paintings of the life of St Benedict in the coffered ceiling of the chancel.

Louriçal

Soure

Louriçal and Soure are two towns of interest between the main road south from Coimbra, and a highway from Figueira da Foz to Leiria. Louriçal has a large, very late 17th century convent, again occupied by a community of Poor Clare nuns. Soure possesses a ruined castle and a lovely Misericordia church, with a particularly fine, painted, wooden barrel ceiling.

Lorvão

A lovely road east of Coimbra curves above the Mondego, through splendid wooded country to the great Cistercian monastery of Lorvão. Lying at the bottom of a long valley, the village nestles up to the great façade of the convent buildings, which are now a psychiatric hospital. The classical church is large and conventional, but the bronze and iron grille to the choir is superb. The two storeyed cloister is pretty and the small museum off the sanctuary is well worth seeing. A portable organ, paintings and vestments including a unique ciborium veil embroidered by the nuns in gold on white with a lamb and a pelican in solid pearls, form part of the collection.

Bussaco
Palace Hotel

North of Lorvão, the *Palace Hotel of Bussaco* is in the centre of the great forest, now a National Park. It is one of the most notable hotels in Europe. Built at the end of the last century as a royal palace, in a neo-Manueline style, the building was turned into a luxury hotel after the departure of the last King of Portugal in 1910. The 80 rooms are large and very comfortable, the public rooms magnificent and there is an excellent restaurant.

Forest

The forest was the property of different religious orders from as early as the 6th century and in 1628, the Discalced Carmelite friars built a monastery, the remains of which are near the hotel, and surrounded the great area by a wall. It was they who planted the famous cypresses of Bussaco, acquiring the seeds from another community in Mexico. Their rarity and great beauty have made them famous to botanists and sylviculturalists all over the world. The hillsides are clothed with luxuriant masses of cork oaks, mimosa, tree heaths, maples and great forest trees which are carefully tended by the Forestry Commission, so that to-day the 250 enclosed acres of woodland include every native variety of tree as well as about 300 exotic varieties.

Here, in September 1810, Wellington again faced the French, who were under the command of Massena. After several attacks the Anglo-Portuguese troops forced the French troops down the hill and the battle was won. To this day, Napier's 'Peninsular War' is one of the best guides to this extraordinary place, intersected by walks leading to fountains, lakes, waterfalls and shrines. Outside the main gate there is a small military museum, featuring the Peninsular War and the Battle of Bussaco which is commemorated by a tall obelisk nearby.

A road north from Figueira da Foz to Aveiro, runs alongside lagoons and watery marshes by the sea. Tocha, the first place of any size, is typical of this coastal country where most of the houses are made of mud bricks, hardened in the sun. *Tocha*

Mira, the next town, got its name from the Arab occupation, Mira being a corruption of the word 'Emir'. A road from here to the sea leads to a village called Palheiros de Mira – '*palha*' is the Portuguese word for straw – many of the cottage walls of which are reinforced with straw owing to the lack of more durable material. *Mira*

Palheiros de Mira

Slightly to the north-west of Mira, through Vagos, are the fascinating porcelain works of Vista Alegre. The factory, which still produces lovely ornaments and table services, was founded by José Ferreira Pinto Basto in 1824, in the large property which gave its name to the porcelain. The clay, suitable for producing hard-paste porcelain, similar to that of Berlin, comes from near Ovar to the north. The factory is still in the hands of the founder's family. He created an early example of intelligent town planning in the streets of pretty houses, each with a garden, for the workers. Many of the present workers are descended from the original craftsmen. This village has a health centre, schools and every kind of amenity. The porcelain works are elegantly housed around a large tree-covered space, with a museum of almost all the different patterns produced over the years. This is open every afternoon from 14.30 to 18.00, except on Saturdays, Sundays and public holidays. There is also a small shop selling examples of the ware. *Vista Alegre Porcelain Works*

The chapel of the Quinta, which originally belonged to the Bishop of Miranda, is a highly decorated late 17th century building with the fantastic tomb of the founder, by the French sculptor Claude Laprade. The altars are splendid Baroque pieces and the sacristy is also magnificently decorated.

North of Vista Alegre, the town of Ilhavo contains a country museum, devoted mainly to objects connected with the sea and with fishing. There is one room of early Vista Alegre porcelain as well as collections of sea shells and local costumes, which have now disappeared from almost every part of the country. The four star *Albergaria Arimar*, with a restaurant, is very comfortable. *Ilhavo*

Aveiro
Aveiro, with good hotels and pensions and excellent restaurants,

many specialising in sea food, would be an original and amusing place in which to stay for a few days while exploring this part of the Gold Coast, above Coimbra and Figueira da Foz. The best hotel is the three star *Imperial*.

The railway station, like many in Portugal, is adorned with diverting Edwardian tiled pictures. The main line runs north to Oporto.

Salt Pans

On the estuary of the river Vouga, Aveiro was an important port in the Middle Ages until a violent storm in 1575 closed the entrance with vast banks of sand. It is now regaining its activities as a port and there are large shipbuilding and fishing industries. The city is protected from the sea by long dunes and saltings and the only opening through to the ocean is at the Praia de Barra. Round the city are an infinite number of salt pans, traversed by long, low bridges on stilts, some of which are suitable for cars. In the late summer, the salt is gathered into pyramids which glisten white in the sun, and those that are not going to be used immediately, are thatched with straw against the winter storms.

Lagoon

The long seawater lagoon, the Ria de Aveiro, stretches for miles. The *Pousada da Ria* (tel. (0034) 48332), is 40 miles away by road, on a peninsula, separating from the Atlantic this strange watery world given over to birds and fish, and the local people to whom these lonely spaces are home. Motorboats can be hired to explore the lagoon, by application to the tourist office in Aveiro.

Moliceiros, as the local boats are called, are unusual and beautiful with high swan-neck prows, painted in bright colours with rustic designs. These boats carry long rakes for collecting the seaweed which is used as fertilizer. The fishing boats are rather different and punts are also employed for laying down nets, as much of the lagoon is very shallow and teeming with fish.

Museum

The museum, made famous by Sacheverell Sitwell in several of his books, is in the former Convent of Jesus, originally built in the 15th century. Princess Joanna, daughter of King Afonso V, became a nun in the convent. Her extraordinary portrait, looking full face out of the canvas, shows Joanna, still dressed as a princess, with a jewelled Renaissance headdress coming down over her forehead, her chestnut hair falling over her shoulders and arms. The face is so singular that one feels it must be an authentic portrait.

The museum is large, for the golden shrines and chapel of the convent can all be visited. In the chapel, which is completely covered with the finest Baroque gold work, there is a delightful series of 17th century canvases showing the princess leaving her father's house, her entry into the convent, her life there and holy death. The museum also contains superb polychrome carved wood statues and shrines as well as some fine primitive paintings.

Cloister, Vila Nova de Gaia

Oporto and Environs

Oporto

The capital of the north of Portugal is not only the home of port wine but is also a big commercial and industrial city. Spread along the northern banks of the Douro, Oporto is now built right up to Foz do Douro, at the mouth of the river. Since pre-Christian times, there has been a settlement on this site and it later became a stronghold of Christianity under the Barbarian and Moorish invasions. The Romans called the city Portucale, which later gave its name to the whole country. After Afonso Henriques established the country's independence in 1139, the town grew in size and became known by its present Portuguese name of Porto.

The great gorge through which the Douro, the river of gold, runs, is spanned by three bridges. The upper is the Dona Maria Pia, designed by Eiffel a century ago. The graceful span carries the railway across to the main station, Campanhã. The middle bridge is the Dom Luiz, built shortly after the Maria Pia, with two road-

Bridges

ways, the top linking the upper part of the city with Vila Nova de Gaia on the south side, in which are all the port wine lodges; the lower leading from Oporto to the lodges actually on the river, which facilitated transport in former days when the casks of untreated wine came down in special boats from the vineyards.

The Arrabida bridge is the furthest downstream, and carries the main highway from Lisbon into the city and the new circular road surrounding it. This bridge, built in 1953, is supported on a single, reinforced, concrete span, almost 900 ft in length, one of the longest in the world.

A riverside road has been constructed in recent years, destroying many of the overcrowded slum dwellings which had existed for centuries on the banks of the river.

Lisbon and Oporto are utterly different, in feel, in architecture and even in the inhabitants. Oporto is fundamentally a commercial city and oddly enough, has been a centre of revolutionary movements from the time of the Liberal uprising of 1820, though the Revolution of 1974 was conceived and carried out by the army in Lisbon.

Oporto is essentially an 18th century town, owing to its great economic development in that century after the Methuen Treaty of 1703 between England and Portugal. This treaty provided for the exchange of English goods, especially wool, for the wines from the Upper Douro. A trading centre was established by English merchants in 1717 and gradually English companies gained control over the production of port wine. The visitor will discover that Oporto is not an easy city to find one's way about, so it is fortunate that the main buildings of interest are all concentrated in an area of a little over a square mile. The density of traffic and the proliferation of one-way streets makes it very much easier for the energetic sightseer to go on foot than to attempt to drive a car in this congested centre of the city. There are plenty of taxis and buses.

Torre dos
Clerigos

The city is dominated by the elegant Torre dos Clerigos, the highest tower in Portugal, which was built by the Italian architect, Nicolas Nazzoni, in the mid 18th century. The tower is open to visitors and an amazing panorama can be seen from the top. The church below is charming, oval in shape which is unusual, and contains lovely fittings.

St Anthony's
Hospital

A little way to the west, towards the mouth of the river, is the great façade of St Anthony's Hospital, which was built between 1770 and 1795 by the English architect, John Carr of York, who had previously designed Harewood House. The large, new hospital of São João is in the suburbs, but St Anthony's has been modernised behind its formal façade and is still in use. Between the hospital and the university, are two Carmelite churches side by side, one with a huge tiled pictorial composition covering an exterior wall.

112

Behind the hospital, in the Rua D. Maria II, the Soares dos Reis Museum is open daily except Mondays, from 10.00 to 17.00, as are most other museums, though some shut for lunch. The Palacio das Carrancas, in which the museum is housed, is a good example of mid-18th century domestic architecture. The collections are very fine, including early French, Italian, Flemish and Portuguese paintings, and later works by Pillement, Quillard and Tenier: Soares dos Reis, who gives his name to the museum, was the most notable Portuguese sculptor of the last century and many of his works, including the enigmatic bust of the 'English Lady', Mrs Leech, are shown. The collection of early ceramics is one of the best in Portugal, with not only pieces from other parts of Europe, but also the productions of Portuguese 18th century pottery factories, in Lisbon, Mafra, Coimbra and Viana do Castelo, which are little known outside the country. The early jewellery and gold and silver work are of great interest. *Soares dos Reis Museum*

Not far from the Soares dos Reis museum, near the Palacio Cristal, rebuilt as a sports centre after a fire, down the leafy Rua de Entre Quintas, the city council have installed an enchanting Romantic museum in the Quinta da Macieirinha, (shut from 12.30 to 14.00). The house is filled with Regency and early-Victorian furniture and ornaments that belonged to the exiled King Charles Albert of Sardinia who, after his abdication, sought refuge in this house in 1849. The gardens are particularly beautiful and filled with rare camelias, for which Oporto is famous, and other specimens. *Quinta da Macieirinha Museum*

On the higher level of the city, near the upper road across the Dom Luiz bridge, is the Sé, or Cathedral. Fundamentally Romanesque, the church and the cloister have been greatly altered by unsympathetic restoration. However, there is a splendid, solid silver reredos altar and tabernacle in the Blessed Sacrament Chapel, which was whitewashed in the Peninsular War so that marauding soldiers would not realise its value. The choir stalls should be noticed. The sacristy walls are covered with good 17th and 18th century canvases in rococo gold frames and superb vestment chests stand below. Off the Gothic cloister, there are some elegant chapels with good *azulejos* and in the Chapel of St Vincent, an unusual set of polychrome bas reliefs can be seen. *Cathedral*

At one side of the great paved space in front of the cathedral, which overlooks the river and the lower part of the city, is the former episcopal palace, now used as municipal offices. The long Baroque façade, with elegant granite surrounds and pediments to the windows, is particularly satisfying. *Bishop's Palace*

By the cathedral, at 32, Rua de Dom Ugo, the Guerra Junqueiro museum is in this well-known Portuguese poet's own house, open from 14.00 to 18.00. The house, given to the City Fathers by the widow and daughter of the poet, still seems more like a loved home than a museum. There is beautiful furniture, fine table silver, tapestries, porcelain, sculpture and even Nottingham alabasters. *Guerra Junqueiro Museum*

Santa Clara Church

On the other side of the main road, the church of Santa Clara, in the Largo de Santa Clara, though Romanesque outside possesses some of the best Baroque gold work in the country. The church is like a golden cave, the ceiling studded with gold bosses and the chancel, including the ceiling, is completely covered with golden angels and cherubs amid formal leaves and patterns. The polychrome statues are superb and there is a pair of tiny organs. Ask the Sacristan, or whoever is around, to take you into the choirs behind the grilles at the end of the church. They have beautiful painted ceilings, carved choirstalls with heads of people and of dogs under the seats and old canvases.

Ethnographic Museum

Between the upper level and the waterfront, the Ethnographic Museum, in the Largo São João Novo, is housed in another 18th century town house. The contents consist of examples of the arts and handicrafts of the Douro, as well as Roman coins and other archaeological remains. There is local earthenware, gold filigree work, models, dolls in regional costume and whole rooms removed from old houses.

São Francisco Church

The oldest part of Oporto is down by the river below the escarpment on which the cathedral is built. The church of São Francisco is a 14th century Gothic building, which was completely lined with the richest Baroque woodwork in the 17th and 18th centuries. Even the pillars and the ceiling are covered with gold work, making an extraordinary conglomeration with, every now and then, an austere Gothic shape emerging through the gilded richness.

British Factory House

Also on this level is the Rua do Infante Henrique, where Queen Philippa of Lancaster gave birth to Prince Henry the Navigator. In the same street is the magnificent British Factory House. In the 16th and 17th centuries, English merchants started commercial associations in many cities of importance, and there were several such institutions in Portugal.

The Factory House in Oporto was built in 1785 by William Whitehead, the then British Consul, and it is still owned and run by the English port wine firms, of which the leading members meet there for lunch. They can invite visitors on certain days and it is a rare experience to sit at the large dining-room table, with the members and their guests, eating the good fare provided. After the meal, the members go into an adjoining room to drink their port so that the savour of the wine is not affected by the smell of food. The rooms in the Factory House are beautifully proportioned, with contemporary furniture, huge crystal chandeliers and painted ceilings.

Accommodation

There are two luxury hotels in Oporto, the *Infante de Sagres* in the Praça D. Philippa de Lencastre which provides the visitor with solid comfort, large bedrooms and excellent food, and the *Porto Atlantico* which is the latest and the most modern. First class hotels include the *Dom Henrique*, in an octagonal tower, with a 15th floor restaurant; the *Castor* in the Rua das Doze Casas 17, is highly

114

recommended by clients; the *Batalha* and the *Grande* are both comfortable and old-fashioned places in the central part of the city. There are numerous *albergarias*, in which only breakfast is served and naturally, large numbers of pensions and boarding houses.

The most famous restaurant in Oporto is the *Escondidinho*, Rua Passos Manuel 144, which specialises in regional food, as well as in real French cooking. But, like Lisbon, Oporto is filled with restaurants at all prices, which are now legally obliged to put their menus with the prices in the windows, so visitors can easily see what they will be charged. *Dobrada*(tripe) with chick peas, or dried beans with chicken and smoked sausage, are local specialities.

Oporto has very good shops on all the main streets; particularly reasonable in price compared to equivalents in other European capitals, are silver work and jewellery. Gold and silver-plated filigree pieces are a speciality of the local artisans and there are also smart locally made shoes, woollens, handbags, baskets and wood and copper work.

Shops

The Rua das Flores near the São Bento station, contains a delight-ful medley of shops as well as the Misericordia church. In the Board Room at the side hangs one of the great artistic treasures of Portugal – the '*Fons Vitae*', an early Flemish painting of Christ on the Cross between the Blessed Virgin and St John, above the kneeling figures of King Manuel I and his wife and children, all clad in violent colours. It is an unforgettable picture.

Fons Vitae

South of Oporto

On the south bank of the Douro, Vila Nova de Gaia is the capital of port wine. The Wine Lodges of the great port firms are strung along the river bank. Wine from the *Pais do Vinho*, – where the small blue grapes are grown on schist, the only grapes which are suitable for making this delectable drink – is brought down by road to the Lodges; after being 'cut' at intervals with brandy, which stops further fermentation, it rests and matures in huge casks. Finally, after continuous blending and treatment, sometimes lasting for years in the case of vintage ports, the wine is ready for dispatch to the many countries to which it is exported. It is a curious fact that port wine is not much drunk in its country of origin, except among foreigners.

Vila Nova de Gaia

Vintage Port

Visitors are admitted to some of the Wine Lodges; inquiries should be made at the tourist office in Oporto, and all types of port can be tried at the Solar do Vinho do Porto in the Rua de Entre Quintas, on the north side of the river. A visit to one of the Wine Lodges is a fascinating experience – walking between the enormous casks, far higher than a man, seeing the bottling process for the finer wines and the rooms where the tasting and blending are carried out. The Lodges are kept at an even temperature and there is an unmistake-

Wine Lodges

able scent in the air of wood from the casks and the fumes from the wine.

The upper level of the Dom Luiz road bridge leads directly to the clifftop above the Wine Lodges. The church and convent of Nossa Senhora do Pilar stands up to the left. The octagonal church, with a beautiful dome, contains elegant statues but what is unique is the circular cloister behind the church, supported on Ionic columns below a highly decorated pediment. From the large terrace outside there is a wonderful view of the city and it was on the slopes below, that Wellington collected his troops before attacking Oporto.

Nossa Senhora do Pilar

Some nine miles south of Vila Nova de Gaia, near the village of Carvalhos, is the ancient monastery of Grijó with a classical 17th century church which has Baroque altars. The 16th century double cloister in the monastery is unusual in its height and the fact that between the two storeys are panels of *azulejos* in carpet pattern, interspersed with tiled pictures of saints; in the centre of the cloister garth is a lovely classical fountain.

Grijó

Both north and south of Oporto there is a series of delightful beaches. But the full force of the Atlantic often makes bathing unsafe, so every resort has one or more swimming pool. To the south, Miramar has a good nine-hole golf course right on the sea and a charming small hotel on the seafront, the *Mirasol*.

Beaches

Further south, towards Espinho, there is a big sandy beach at Granja, with a swimming pool and restaurant beside it.

Twelve miles south of Oporto, Espinho, with another long wide beach, has become a modern resort. There is a casino, open from 15.00 to 03.00 with roulette, French bank and slot machines. Also a restaurant and cabaret. Take your passport, as to all casinos. There are good camp sites in the pinewoods, close to the beach, tennis courts and a big swimming pool. A mile to the south is one of the best 18-hole golf courses in the country, Europe's second oldest golf course, (the first was in Pau in the French Pyrenees) which was started in 1890 by British port wine shippers. There is a club house and those staying at the hotel on the beach, the four star *Praia Golfe*, pay no green fees. The *Hotel de Espinho* and the *Mar Azul*, are smaller and more intimate and there are several pensions and restaurants.

Espinho Casino

Golf

Three miles south of Espinho, between Paramos and Esmoriz, there is a lagoon with excellent sailing, swimming and rowing facilities. The lagoon is surrounded by groves of pines and other trees, making ideal camping grounds.

Lagoon

A few miles south-east of Espinho, the town of Vila da Feira possesses a romantic castle with pepperpot turrets set within an oval barbican, on the side of a hill against a background of tall old trees, looking not unlike a castle in a fairy tale. The interior is

Vila da Feira

116

divided into three floors to which the visitor can ascend. At one end of the encircling battlements is a small octagonal chapel with a little house clinging snail-like to one side.

The town of Feira is pretty, with old houses and a church with a façade of powder-blue tiles. This is part of the monastery of the Holy Spirit which belonged to the Canons Regular of St John the Baptist, who were familiarly known as the Blue Canons, which may have been the reason why this church was so elegantly ornamented.

The Misericordia has a good Baroque retable and a very odd statue of St Christopher in a chapel off the side entrance. This stands 12 foot high, with a huge bearded painted face above a red robe and the wooden hands are articulated at the wrists. The statue was formerly carried through the town in procession.

Due east of Vila da Feira, but actually reached by a turning to the East in São João da Madeira, is the superb convent of Arouca. The small town is immensely ancient, set in a wide valley between distant mountains and dominated by the convent, which owed its grandeur to the Queen, Santa Mafalda, formerly wife of Henry I of Castille, who retired here several years before her death in 1256. The elegant 18th century buildings are now a Salesian boys' school. They enclose several courtyards and a late double cloister, off which is a chapter house surrounded by early 18th century polychrome tiled panels of country scenes.

Arouca

Convent

The museum (open from 10.00 to 12.00 and 14.00 to 18.00), contains fascinating pieces including some very good Portuguese primitives, a moving 17th century bas-relief of St Teresa of Avila, a lovely panel of St Bernard surrounded by Cistercian monks and nuns, a 16th century statue of St Roque with his dog, a pre-historic gold bracelet and amusing things like an 18th century doll's study in a glass case with miniature furniture, pictures and bird cages and an Abbess's chair with a high oval back, somewhat like the Bishop's chair in Faro museum. These valuable possessions were going to be dispersed after the Revolution in 1910, but the towns-people and the Confraternity which had charge of them utterly refused to let them go.

Museum

The church has good canvases in Baroque frames in the chancel and early statues in the retable of the high altar. Unique are the great 18th century standing stone statues of Cistercian nuns, in formal pleated habits, and with delicately pink cheeks and lips, which look down from high up on the walls of the nuns' choir. There is a particularly lovely organ of the same period and no less than 104 choir stalls backed by great rococo panels enclosing 18th century canvases.

Church

This touchingly rustic Misericordia is in a pretty square outside the convent. The coffered ceiling is inset with panels of saints ex-

Misericordia

117

ecuted by some journeyman painter and the walls are covered with carpet *azulejos*.

There is a *Residencia* in the town and the *Pension Alexandre* provides simple food.

North of Oporto

Leça do Bailio

North of Oporto and almost in the suburbs, on the way to the airport, Leça do Bailio is noted for a fine Templars church, with a castellated tower. The three-aisled Gothic interior, has a noble sobriety. Not far away is the lovely Quinta do Chantre, a typical Portuguese country house designed by Nazzoni in the mid 18th century, a double staircase reaching to the main doorway on the first floor, which is surmounted by a tower with a coat-of-arms emblazoned on the façade.

Matosinhos

Matosinhos has a small beach, slightly away from the town, with complete camping facilities and particularly good seafood restaurants. At Whitsun, there is a big fair and pilgrimage to the church of Bom Jesus, a bizarre 18th century building in which a very ancient statue of Christ is revered. The woodwork in this church is notable.

Although there are side roads by the coast, with several almost deserted beaches, the main road north to Vila do Conde is a few miles inland.

Vila do Conde

Vila do Conde, near the mouth of the Rio Ave, was once noted for its shipyards. Now, only a few wooden-hulled ships for the inshore fishing trade are made every year by craftsmen using the same kind of tools that their forebears worked with, but this is a dying craft. The town is still, fortunately, a centre for a more delicate type of handicraft, that is lace-making. The lace-making school, Escola de Rendas, at Rua Joaquim Maria de Melo 70, welcomes visitors and most beautiful examples of the work can be bought. The lacemakers come into their own on the Feast of St John and on the nights of June 23rd and 24th, cross the town, floodlit for the occasion, and go down to the beach escorted by most of the inhabitants.

Lace-making

Convent and Church of St Clare

Vila do Conde is bright with flowers and shaded by masses of trees. Reflected in the placid waters of the river is the huge Convent of St Clare, now a charitable home, towering above a row of low houses. The Gothic church of the convent has remained intact but unhappily, in the restorations of some 45 years ago, the roof of the beautiful cloister was removed for no apparent reason. So now the delicate arches stand desolate around a bare courtyard in which is a Renaissance fountain, originally the terminal of the long aqueduct, consisting of 999 arches, built in the early 18th century, which brought water to the convent.

There are camping facilities and many restaurants on the beach by the castle at the river mouth, as well as the four star *Estalagem do Brasão.*

Three miles north is Povoa de Varzim, another large seaside resort with a casino for gamblers, and a nightclub and restaurant with dance floor and cabaret. In addition to possessing the longest beach in Portugal of six miles of clean sand, Povoa has a large fishing port at the southern end of the town, and every day, except Saturdays, Sundays and holidays, the catch is auctioned when the boats come in, an interesting and fascinating sight. Fishermen can hire rowing boats for inshore fishing and motorboats for the offshore. There are quantities of sea bass to be caught, some weighing over 20 pounds. Sailing on a large lagoon is also available.

Povoa de Varzim

Beach

Fishing

The *Hotel Vermar Dom Pedro* is in the first-class category, with two heated swimming pools, one for children, just above the beach. There is a good grill-room and restaurant. The *Grande Hotel da Povoa*, slightly less expensive, is also on the sea front, with a bar and snack-bar, and there are several estalagems. The restaurants are good and the shops exceptional, many specialising in the locally hand-knitted fishermen's sweaters, pottery and filigree work. A gold and silversmiths called Gomes, in the Rua Junqueira, is worth going to, for the silversmith's work behind a glass partition, so that visitors can observe their fascinating expertise.

Accommoda-tion

The local museum of Ethnography and History, has recently received the Special Exhibitions Award, given by the Bank of Ireland, in connection with the European Museums of the Year awards.

Ethnography Museum

A couple of miles to the north of Povoa, A Ver o Mar, a village with a lovely beach, is the scene of an unusual agricultural experiment. The local farmers dug deep into the sand dunes until they came to moist ground. The sides of these depressions have been shored up by grape vines giving a good crop of grapes which, as may be imagined, taste very different from those grown in more conventional soils. Many types of vegetables, including potatoes, sweet corn and cabbages flourish in small plots, divided up like allotments, apparently fertilised by the saline water at their roots. This strange area surrounds the excellent four star *Estalagem de S. André*, which has a discotheque as well as a restaurant with notably good food.

A Ver o Mar

Accommoda-tion

Early Romanesque churches are to be found at Rio Mau and Rates on the road north to Vila Nova de Famalicão; the former dates from 1151, while the latter, São Pedro de Rates, is slightly later in date and is the more interesting, the exterior of the chancel being semi-circular, with arches surrounding the lancet windows. The three-aisled interior, separated by rounded arches supported on heavy columns, is almost French in feeling.

Rio Mau

São Pedro de Rates

119

All around Oporto, and in the Minho province to the north, there are numbers of these early-Romanesque churches, most of which have been much over-restored. What is unique in the north, as in other parts of the country, is the large number of Rococo and Baroque churches and buildings, with a typically Portuguese gaiety of spirit.

Guimarães Castle

The Minho

The main city of the northern part of the country is Braga, out of which six main roads radiate starwise. Two lead to that part of the Minho which goes, wedge-shaped up to the Spanish frontier, one leads to the sea at Esposende through Barcelos, one down to Oporto, one to Lamego through Guimarães and the other, a very mountainous road, east through Chaves to Bragança in Tras-os-Montes, the extreme north-eastern part of Portugal. The railway runs up to the frontier at Valença do Minho.

Braga

Braga is not an easy place in which to get one's bearings. Large new highways have been built around the original centre of this very ancient town. The Goths are known to have been there in 584, and the Moors destroyed the city 150 years later. In 1040, just before the Norman Conquest, the city was taken by the Castilians when the Bishopric was restored, and the Archbishop of Braga is still the Primate of Portugal. The splendour of the Renaissance buildings in the town is due to Archbishop Diogo de Sousa who ruled for over 20 years from 1508 and, two centuries later, Dom Rodrigo de Moura Teles and Dom Gaspar de Bragança, made their Episcopal city into the centre of Portuguese Baroque art.

Cathedral	The cathedral is a strange mixture of styles; the original edifice, of which little remains, was started in 1070. The main portal and the apse are flamboyant Gothic and the Manueline carved stone frontal of the high altar is all that is left of the original Manueline retable, torn out in the 18th century when the Baroque choir stalls, splendid organs and other fittings, were installed.

A chapel to the right of the entrance contains the canopied tomb, like a fourposter bed, of Afonso, son of King John I and Philippa of Lancaster, who died as a young man in 1400.

Museum	The museum, well worth seeing, is off the cloisters, to the left of the cathedral. Like most country museums in Portugal, it is the more interesting for containing a large agglomeration of objects, from a very early metal crucifix and a quite lovely 14th century crystal cross set in bronze, to superb church vessels, many of pure gold, and fine 18th-century vestments.

The main façade of the cathedral is approached by a street with very pretty old houses on either side, one of which is covered with elegant green tiles, and all of which have good ironwork balconies. At the extreme back of the apse, there is a beautiful late-Gothic statue of Our Lady suckling the Holy Child, which is attributed to Nicolas Chantarene who did so much sculpture in the north of Portugal, and there is a very early Gothic house nearby.

Misericordia	The Misericordia church in the street behind the cathedral cloister, is a riot of golden Baroque, which fills the whole of the wall behind the high altar, enclosing an elegant early-Victorian painting of Our Lady of Mercy, her cloak spread out to shelter those seeking help. A little further down, this street is spanned by a particularly lovely Renaissance arch, and there is another fine arch over the Rua S. Geraldo.

Coimbras Chapel	A short walk from the cathedral, in a pleasant square, stands the castellated Coimbras chapel, a tiny Gothic edifice in which three lovely polychrome stone saints and 18th century tiles can be seen through a grille. A very early Manueline house still used as a dwelling, with shops below, should be noted. A couple of hundred yards further on is the magnificent façade of the São Marcos
Hospital	hospital with full-size statues of saints standing on the pediment. Down the street, to the left of the hospital, the Casa do Raio was
Casa do Raio	built in the middle of the 18th century, in the full flush of Portuguese Baroque. The windows are surrounded by ornate granite carvings, set within the façade of powder blue tiles. On the balustraded pediment stand urns with flambeaux and, separating the ground from the first floor, is a long balcony of very fine ironwork.

Accommodation	In this square is the *Estalagem de S. Geraldo*, a good place to stay, as it is within walking distance of the main sights of the city.

On the Avenida Central, a long pleasant public park, with plenty of benches in the shade, is the chapel of Penha de França. This tiny building is blessedly untouched, filled with golden Baroque altars, a glorious pulpit with an archangel standing on top of the sounding board, and 18th century pictorial tiled panels right up to the plain ceiling, but as has already been said, Braga is the main centre of Portuguese Baroque art, and almost every church in the city has features of interest.

Penha de França Chapel

Also on the Avenida Central, at number 1 is the comfortable and very moderate *Hotel Francfort* with a good restaurant.

The Biscainhas museum is installed in one of the fine granite and whitewashed town houses in which Braga abounds. It contains agreeable furniture, silver, china, pottery, and particularly lovely decorative tiles line the walls, as they do the elegant, formal garden.

Biscainhas Museum

Just outside Braga, an immensely tall flight of monumental steps, broken at intervals, like those of Nossa Senhora dos Remédios at Lamego, by landings with chapels, leads up to the church of Bom Jesus in a lovely setting of great woods. On the same level is a good four star hotel, the *Elevador*, and two or three lesser, but perfectly viable hostelries.

Bom Jesus Church

Accommodation

On the same side of the city of Braga, on another spur of the same range of hills, at Falperra, is one of the strangest rococo churches in the whole of Portugal. Santa Maria Madalena is not easy to see as a whole, as there is a series of steps up to the church, of which the wild granite ornamentation conceals almost the whole of the whitewashed façade. The octagonal interior is high with a tall blue and gold retable and fine chandeliers. On a lower level from this church, around which hoopoes and a great variety of birds dart in and out of the woods, is a long, low building with a restaurant at one end. The other part, once a seminary, now houses '*retornados*' from the former Portuguese possessions in Africa.

Santa Maria Madalena

Not far from Falperra, behind Sameiro, are the remains of the most important Castro, or hill city, in Portugal. The Citania de Briteiros is an Iron Age fortified city on a hill, covering several acres. There are three outer walls, paved roadways, water tanks and channels for the water supply, as well as circular and rectangular houses. Many of the archaeological remains from Briteiros are in the Martins Sarmento museum at Guimarães, including some unique objects. Visitors to Portugal who are interested in the Iron Age and Celtic civilizations should make a special point of visiting at least one of these *citanias*, of which there is another nearby, at Sabroso.

Citania de Briteiros

At the other extremity of Braga, the road to Ponte de Lima reaches, in a couple of miles, the village of São Jeronimo Real in which is a sign saying 'São Frutuoso'. This Byzantine chapel, originally built between 650 and 655, is unique in Portugal. It is in the form of a Greek cross with a central dome and rich carving round the angles

São Frutuoso

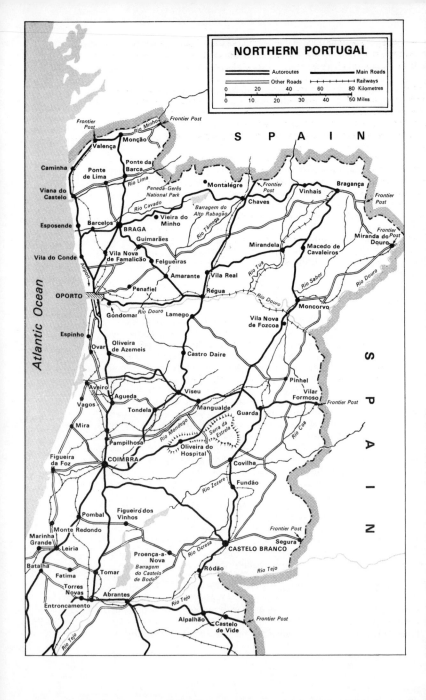

between the arches and on the capitals of the pillars. To one side, in strange contrast, is a Franciscan Baroque church with beautiful fittings, green, black and gold choir stalls and a superb sacristy.

On the other side of the main road, a turning leads to the immense, derelict Benedictine monastery of Tibães. It is approached by a flight of steps below which is a beautiful village cross. Most of the ruined buildings are privately owned, but the parish priest lives in part of them so the key to the marvellous church is available. *Monastery of Tibães*

The great church is filled with wonderful luminous gold work, in admirable condition. The windows are surmounted by golden pelmets and gold surrounds and there is a pair of very fine ambones. Two giant-faced satyrs support the organ, which is topped by elegant statues. The choir stalls in the chancel are backed by unusual golden whorls and the Baroque high altar encloses very fine 17th century polychrome carved wooden statues of St Benedict and other saints. In the first chapel to the right there is a polychrome carved group of the Holy Family and below, in a smaller Rococo shrine, Our Lady is showing the Holy Child to St Joseph.

Barcelos

A road due east from Braga leads to Barcelos and the sea at Esposende, and a side road from Tibães joins this main road. Barcelos is one of the prettiest towns in Portugal, descending to the river Cavado, crossed by a 14th century bridge. The town is not large, so visitors can easily explore it on foot. The great feature of the place is the Campo da Feira, or fairground, with shady trees and a Renaissance fountain in the centre. The huge space is surrounded on two sides by lovely conventual buildings – to the west is a row of elegant 18th century houses, while the south side is filled by an elaborate granite parapet adorned with fountains and obelisks overlooking a public garden, the flowerbeds all in Baroque shapes to follow the architecture of the town. In the south-west corner of the Campo da Feira, by this elegant conceit, is the octagonal church of Senhor da Cruz, brilliantly whitewashed behind granite columns supporting an ornate balustrade and belfry. The granite dome is supported within the church on great flat columns, and there are fine blue 18th century *azulejos* panels on the walls. Two angels, in strange 18th century costume, stand on either side of the high altar, and the two deeply-recessed side altars are lined with golden woodwork. The pale gold organ loft should be noticed. *Fairground*

Senhor da Cruz Church

On the north side of the Campo da Feira, stands the extremely interesting church of St Benedict, now known as the Terço. Plain outside, the interior of the church is lined with two rows of superb *azulejos* panels, illustrating the life of St Benedict, right up to the coffered ceiling which has a series of 55 exceptionally good paintings. They have been well restored, making this ceiling one of the *Terço Church*

125

finest of its period in the country. Below the large tiled pictures of Benedictines, one with the monks sitting at a refectory table, not unlike the composition of the great Zuberan canvas in Seville, there are small tiled panels each picturing, in an amusing way, an aphorism suited to the religious life.

Fair
On Thursdays, an enormous fair is held in the Campo da Feira, which is then entirely covered with stalls selling produce, kitchen ware and pottery, so that no overall view of this lovely space is possible. Even on fair days there is plenty of parking in the town.

Handicraft Centre
Visitors wishing to buy the local brightly hand-painted pottery, including the Barcelos cock, stemming from a medieval legend, can buy it both at the tourist office opposite Senhor da Cruz, open from 09.30 to 12.00 and 14.00 to 17.30, and at the Centro de Artesenato and museum in the square below the fine 18th century town hall.

Archaeo-logical Museum
To the west, and actually on top of the handicraft centre, is a very early Gothic church, surrounded by an open-air museum of archaeological remains reaching up to the ruined Paço dos Condes.

There are several restaurants and the four star *Albergaria Condes de Barcelos* for overnight stays.

Due west of Barcelos are two well-known watering places, Esposende, on the north bank of the Cavado estuary, and Ofir to the south.

Esposende
Esposende is an old fishing village, with some fine early buildings, whose busy life, and that of its fishermen, goes on unaffected by the tourists who stay in the comfortable hotels, the *Nélia* and the *Suave Mar* and bathe from the wide beach.

Ofir

Sport
Ofir has several luxury hotels, including the four star *Ofir* and *Pinhal* by the immensely long, sandy beach, as well as accommodation of a simpler type, including a good camping site. Sailing or rowing boats can be hired and water skiing, as well as sea fishing, tennis and riding are available. There is also a ten-pin bowling alley, one of the only two in Portugal, and a golf course is being planned.

Fão
Just south of Ofir, the village of Fão dates back to Roman times, with charming houses. The seaweed gatherers, or *sargaceiros*, are an interesting sight. The men, who wear toga-like costumes, work with two wooden rakes and nets to draw in the seaweed for use as fertiliser.

Viana do Castelo

Some 30 miles north of Esposende, a long bridge crosses the

estuary of the river Lima to Viana do Castelo. The view from the bridge of this ancient city, guarded by the wooded hill of Santa Luzia, with a four star hotel and a basilica on the summit, and a Celtic-Iberian hill city behind, has unhappily been ruined by the erection, just above the town, of a hideous new building of great length. Fortunately, this is not seen from the lovely centre of the town, grouped around the triangular Praça da Republica. At one side is the early town hall, with arches below, and yet another Renaissance fountain stands in the centre. At one side is the extraordinary Misericordia, with a three-tiered façade supported *Misericordia* by granite caryatids. The church has good features of a boldly painted ceiling, *azulejos* panels and a pair of charming organs. It is hoped soon to set up a small museum of the medical bygones, which have been found. These include an unusual windowless sedan chair, in which the very sick were carried to the hospital.

To the west of the town the singular Rococo chapel of Nossa *Nossa* Senhora da Agonia, stands at one end of a large bare space. The *Senhora* interior has pale golden altars, on one of which lies a glass case *da Agonia* containing the waxed-over body of Saint Severino who is dressed in outlandish golden muslin garments with a gaudy turban on his head. One of the biggest *romarias* takes place outside this chapel every August. There is a fair, dancing, bands, processions, fireworks, and general jollifications go on for some days.

The municipal museum is set up in the Barbosa Macieis Palace in *Museum* the Largo de S. Domingos. It is not large but has a notable collection of 18th century Viana pottery, a rare Nottingham alabaster, good furniture, a tiny early Pieta, water colours, wash drawings and prints.

The Viana do Castelo embroidery of flowered patterns on table linen is exported all over the world. The most elegant is the white on white, but it is also made in red and blue on white.

The *Parque* and *Afonso III* are both four star hotels and there are several pensions and restaurants. The road north from Viana do Castelo, runs a short way inland from the sea, with the railway line alongside, to Vila Praia de Ancora at the mouth of the river Ancora. There are sandy beaches, bass fishing from the shore and fly *Beaches* fishing for trout in the river. Accommodation and good restaurants *Fishing* are plentiful.

Just before reaching the estuary of the Minho, forming the frontier with Spain, there is another good beach at Moledo. *Moledo*

Frontier Towns

The delightful fortified town of Caminha is surrounded on three *Caminha* sides by the river and faces the mountains of Galicia, in Spain. Medieval buildings, including the Gothic Pitas Palace, surround the main square with the town hall and clock tower, which was once part of the 14th century fortifications. The granite parish church looks like a fortress and shows definite traces of Spanish, rather than Portuguese, decoration.

Valença do Minho Valença, the frontier post opposite Tuy on the Spanish side has an international road and rail bridge over the river. Within the fortifications crowning a hill, are two separate villages, each within their encircling walls. The houses are charming, bright and covered with flowers and the narrow lanes lead to unexpectedly picturesque corners. At the extreme end of the larger enclosure and overlooking the river, is the luxury *Pousada de São Teotonio* (tel. (0021) 22252), a perfect place to stay for a few days of complete rest, surrounded by superb views. In the town below, some elegant French railway carriages can be seen by the station, with an English Beyer Peacock locomotive, made in Manchester in 1875. These can be hired for organised excursions.

Monção Further up the river, Monção, also a fortified town, with a battlemented tower on the water's edge, is famous for its lampreys which can be eaten in the late winter and early spring. The *Albergaria Atlantico* is first class and there are several restaurants all serving local specialities, which include salmon and trout.

Brejoeira Palace South of Monção is the early 19th century Brejoeira Palace. Modelled on the Ajuda palace in Lisbon, it is the last of the great country houses to be built in Portugal.

Melgaço All the towns and villages on the river Minho are fortified against Spanish aggression which, as indicated, was a constant threat to Portugal through the centuries. Melgaço, well up the river towards the frontier post of São Gregorio, is no exception. The small town contains two Romanesque churches and there are others nearby at Fiães and Paderne.

Castro Laboreiro A road south from Melgaço ends, in some 15 miles, at Castro Laboreiro, home of a special breed of sheepdog. The winding route is extremely beautiful until the distant walls of the tiny city are seen, high above; the countryside is filled with granite *espigueiros*, the stone coffers, on tall struts, in which is stored the winnowed grain after the harvest, so that rats cannot get in to spoil it. These strange edifices are to be found all over the Minho, but nowhere in such numbers as at Castro Laboreiro and Lindoso.

Peneda-Gerês National Park All this part of the frontier is preserved as the National Park of Peneda-Geres and wild boar, wolves, wild horses and civet cats still roam in the heavily wooded valleys and on the bare summits, over which eagles hover.

The best places to stay for this remote and very interesting part of the country, are the luxury *Pousada de São Bento* (tel. (0023) 57190), at Caniçada or in Caldas do Gerês, where there are various hotels and pensions connected with the spa. There is also a camping ground.

On the road south from Monção to Ponte da Barca and Braga, Arcos de Valdevez is a very old town on the river Vez. There are several country houses, churches with beautiful Baroque details and *azulejos* and, in the church of Nossa Senhora da Lapa, built in 1767, one of the oddest Baroque edifices in the country. The exterior consists of a wide oval on to the whitewashed walls of which is attached a two-storied entrance, supported on flat, granite pilasters and surmounted by a waving, pointed cornice and amphorae, as is the roof of the main body of the church. The interior is octagonal, covered by a low, stone dome.

Arcos de Valdevez

The Lima Valley

There are two roads from Viana do Castelo up the river Lima; that on the north bank is the most interesting, passing through wooded countryside to Lanheses with an 18th century country house and, rather further up river, the extraordinary Solar de Bertiandos, actually on the road. This house illustrates the fact that there was a very rapid development in Portugal from late-Gothic architecture through Renaissance to early Baroque. At one side is a 16th century battlemented tower with Gothic steps going down to the forecourt at the side of the main building, which is typical Portuguese late-Renaissance, with an open, columned gallery on the first floor. The square towers at either end, surmounted by obelisks and the windows with plain granite surrounds are all early Baroque. There are many other country houses all around the valley of the river Lima, but few are so visible or so unusual as Bertiando.

Lanheses
Solar de
Bertiandos

The lovely town of Ponte de Lima now has a modern bridge, downstream from the old many-arched, narrow Roman bridge. Over the new bridge stretches a wide walk up the river, shaded by a double avenue of immense plane trees, going up to the old bridge. Two churches, at right angles to each other, São Francisco and Santo Antonio, the latter now having been turned into a museum, are open from 10.00 to 12.00 and 14.00 to 17.30. The former has lovely ambones, fine chandeliers, and a strange image of St George, sitting astride a saddle on a wooden trestle. Behind is a tiny, simple cloister. The town is delightful, prettily whitewashed and with a number of typically 18th century town houses. Little now remains of the walls, but there is a good battlemented tower, once used as the local prison.

Ponte de Lima

Returning to the north bank of the river, from which a lovely view of the town can be seen, over the old bridge to the church of Santo Antonio da Torre Velha, with its elegant onion-topped tower, a gravel road to the right, past a small, square Gothic shrine, leads through a splendid avenue of elms on to the main road, upstream, to Ponte de Barca. This road passes the old Benedictine convent of Refoios do Lima, the monastery being at right angles to the church.

Refoios
do Lima
Convent

The interior has a late-Renaissance retable and, unusually, two side altars are set cornerwise below the chancel arch; the ambones are red and gold and the four side chapels are also elaborately filled with Baroque woodwork and everything that can support a golden pelmet, does so. The convent, now in private hands, is used as a farm and, unlike Tibães, is clearly well managed and conserved. The early 17th century cloister is elegant and the adjoining chapter house still contains unusual polychrome *azulejos* of standing clerical figures, similar to those outside the upper choir of Santa Cruz in Coimbra.

Ponte da
Barca

The road goes on through lovely country to Ponte da Barca, with a famous Gothic bridge across the river. It is an attractive town, much smaller than Ponte de Lima, but with equally fine town houses and a parish church with a groined roof, picked out in gold, and a pair of giant angels standing by the high altar.

Lindoso

From Ponte da Barca, the only road up the Lima goes along a terrifyingly mountainous road to the castellated town of Lindoso, almost on the frontier with Spain. Below the castle the hill is covered with *espigueiros*, ranging in date from the early 18th century to the present day, an extraordinary sight. The low granite houses of the tiny settlement around the castle, look as primitive as some of the Iron Age dwellings of the Citanias of Briteiros and Sabroso near Guimarães.

Rendufe
Monastery

A road due south from Ponte da Barca leads back to Braga. Just before Vila Verde, on this road, a turning to the east goes through Amares, with notable country houses and the monastery of Rendufe a few miles to the south-west. Like so many of these monastic foundations in the north, the buildings are in a terrible state, though the church has been kept up and the Baroque goldwork is almost as fine as that at Tibães.

Santa Maria
de Bouro

The road on from Amares to Geres, a well-known spa, follows a series of long man-made lakes. On this road, which is particularly beautiful, is the Cistercian monastery and church of Santa Maria de Bouro. Yet again, the monastery is largely in ruins, though the church, used as the parish church, is lovely and has good paintings and fine choir stalls. At right angles to the church, on the desolate 17th century façade of the convent, are strange 18th century life-size carved stone statues of five of the kings of Portugal in Shakespearean costumes; as is a group over a doorway of the Holy Family holding hands.

Povoa de
Lanhoso

A road south of the Cavado goes back to Braga through Povoa de Lanhoso, grouped around a high castle springing up from a great rock. On the way up to the fortifications are the remains of circular Iron Age buildings, the Citania de Lanhoso, as well as five little chapels enclosing carved polychrome wooden groups.

Guimarães

Guimarães lies south-east from Braga. Here many of the buildings, unlike those in Braga, have been ruined by over-restoration. The city is the cradle of the Portuguese nation. The first King, Afonso Henriques was born here and baptised in the tiny chapel of São Miguel do Castelo. In Guimarães, Iron Age and Celtic cults preceded the Roman occupation and all left their mark, centuries before the advent of the monarchy.

The Martins Sarmento museum, only open in the afternoon, contains numbers of Iron Age objects, many discovered by Martins Sarmento who, in the latter part of the 19th century, spent his whole life in excavating the Citania de Briteiros. By far the most outstanding exhibit is the Colossus of Pedralva. Only found in Briteiros in 1930, the huge 10-foot-high granite seated statue, was taken to the museum on a specially made vehicle dragged by 24 pairs of oxen. The idol, for such it certainly was, is of the same period as the granite pigs which are found in so many places in Tras-os-Montes. The great arms and legs and powerful, elemental face have an extraordinary vitality and it is strange that although one of the most remarkable prehistoric statues in Europe, it seems to be almost unknown and is barely mentioned even in Portuguese books on Guimarães, though the far less interesting Pedra Formosa, a stone carving also in this museum, has been extensively written about.

Martins Sarmento Museum

Colossus of Pedralva

The Colegiada, or Nossa Senhora de Oliveira, is believed to have been founded in the 11th century, and until comparatively lately, contained lovely things added through the centuries, but now most of these have been removed by some over-zealous so-called expert, who decided to return this famous church to its original appearance. However, the good choir stalls remain and a fine silver tabernacle in a chapel to the right. The sacristy contains six mirrors in lovely frames and off it is a curious cave-like chapel entirely lined with glazed tiles.

Nossa Senhora de Oliveira Church

The church is set in a beautiful square, surrounded by early, arcaded Gothic and Manueline houses and in the open space stands a delightful open-sided Gothic shrine built in 1342 to commemorate a legend that an olive branch put forth leaves when stuck in the ground by Wanda, King of the Goths.

Behind the church, in the Alberto Sampaio museum, are many of the beautiful things taken out of the Colegiada, including Baroque side altars, good canvases, polychrome angels and a splendid six-foot-high Gothic crucifix with silver figures. The most interesting object from the adjoining church is a marvellous 14th century triptych in gold plate of Our Lady lying in bed, grasping the Holy Child by the foot, with Saint Joseph standing at the end of the bed.

Alberto Sampaio Museum

This was given by King John I to the Colegiada in thanksgiving after the Battle of Aljubarrota in 1385. Other exhibits are primitive paintings by Frei Carlos and Antonio Vaz and a lovely 18th century group of Saint Anne and Saint Joachim teaching their little daughter, Mary, to read.

Braganza
Palace
Museum

The third museum in Guimarães is in the restored palace of the Dukes of Braganza, on top of a hill at one side of the city. It contains arms and armour, Chinese porcelain, furniture, very good copies of the Pestrana tapestries in Spain and lovely Persian carpets. The large, cold granite rooms were rebuilt 40 years ago, as only the outer walls of this palace were then standing. The luxury *Pousada de Santa Maria da Oliveira* (tel. (0023) 412157/416554), is in an 18th century palace nearby.

The *Hotel Fundador*, Avenida D. Afonso Henriques 740, is modern and in the new part of town. There are several snack bars in the same street. The *Hotel Toural* at 15 Largo do Toural is pleasant, and the *Milenario* is a good restaurant at number 45 in the same Largo. Guimarães is the centre of the linen trade in Portugal and the Casa dos Linhos, Teixeira de Abreu & Co., is famous for genuine linen by the metre in all widths, as well as made up.

There are several churches in Guimarães, some of which contain interesting features. São Francisco, Gothic in origin, has a Tree of Jesse in high relief and a lovely sacristy, as has the Capuchos church, with agreeable pictures behind the 18th century vestment chests and a coffered ceiling painted with flowers. The 17th century chapel of the Immaculate Conception is another golden cave adorned with contemporary *azulejos* and those who enjoy odd architecture, should seek out the Senhor dos Passos church at the end of a public garden, with a most peculiar Baroque façade.

Nossa
Senhora
do Porto de
Ave

Near Guimarães, at Taide, the shrine of Nossa Senhora do Porto de Ave is most unusual, as the series of monumental granite stairways, interspersed by terraces, fountains, chapels and shrines, statues and great flambeaux against whitewashed plaster walls on either side, lead down to the hexagonal church and not up to it, as in the case of Bom Jesus at Braga and Nossa Senhora dos Remédios at Lamego. All the people from round about come to this shrine for a *romaria* at the beginning of September, still unfrequented by foreigners.

All this part of the Minho, east and north-east of Oporto, is filled with elegant shrines and little chapels, witnesses to the faith that built them.

Amarante

East of Oporto and south-east of Guimarães on the road to Vila Real, lies Amarante on the river Tamega, which is crossed by a Regency bridge. The town is noted for the fair of São Gonçalo on the first weekend in June, when the unmarried girls and young men exchange phallic shaped cakes, thus recalling a fertility cult far earlier than the saint who is regarded locally as the patron of marriages.

Twenty-five km from Amarante, high up in the Serra do Marão, the *Pousada de São Gonçalo* (tel. (0025) 46113), with fantastic views, is a good place for visitors to stay in this somewhat remote part of the country.

Solar de Mateus

Tras-os-
Montes

*Accommoda-
tion*

This north-eastern province of Portugal is little visited by travellers for it is still remote and difficult to reach, and there are few hotels. Fascinating railway routes go from Oporto right up to Chaves, via Vila Real and to Braganza and Miranda do Douro. The main roads to these cities are good but winding and traverse exceptionally beautiful country, high and bare with mountain ranges and groves of sweet chestnut and huge cherry trees. There are good hotels and golf courses at the spas of Vidago and Pedras Salgadas on the way to Chaves; *pousadas* at Braganza and Miranda do Douro, the *Estalagem Santiago* at Chaves, the *Albergaria Cabanelas* at Vila Real and the *Estalagem do Caçador* at Maçedo de Cavaleiros on the way to Braganza, a centre for shooting in the game season. However, every town has reasonably good pensions and the food in the small restaurants is usually excellent.

The distances in Tras-os-Montes are great and the roads, though good, are not geared for fast motoring, so visitors cannot possibly appreciate this little-known part of Europe in a fleeting visit.

Vila Real

The first large town in the province is not far from the *Pousada de São Gonçalo* on the Serra do Marão, already mentioned. The town

134

is filled with 16th and 17th century houses. The cathedral of São Domingos is a Gothic building and the Clerigos church, or Capela Nova, is fan-shaped for it forms the angle between two streets. The Baroque façade is most unusual, two great Tuscan columns standing at each side of the doorway while on the pediment, two archangels clad like Roman Emperors, stand on either side of a statue of St Peter.

A few miles outside the town, towards Braganza, is the most illustrated house in Portugal, for the façade of the Solar de Mateus is reproduced on the label of every bottle of Mateus rosé wine, of which over a million are exported every year. This lovely U-shaped house was built by Nicolas Nazzoni, the architect of so much fine work in Oporto in the first half of the 18th century. The main doorway of the house which is set back from the two wings, is approached by a double staircase. Statuary and a huge coat of arms, with two classical figures at either side, surmount this façade. The absolute symmetry of the building is broken by the chapel with an even more ornate façade, slightly back from the main building. Parts of the interior are shown to the public, with pretty furniture, the original copper blocks of engravings by Fragonard and Gerard, rare books and letters from Wellington, Frederick the Great, Talleyrand and Metternich, among others. *Solar de Mateus*

The first place of any importance on the long haul of 80 miles from Vila Real to Braganza is Murça, noted because it is one of the towns in Tras-os-Montes possessing a pre-historic Iron Age pig carved from granite. The Porca de Murça stands on a plinth in the middle of a public garden, which somewhat takes away from its extreme peculiarity. The pig gives its name to a well known local wine which can be bought all over the country. There is a Gothic figure of St Vincent in the parish church and a tiny Misericordia chapel with a very early Baroque façade adorned with granite Salamonic columns freely carved with grapes and vine leaves as if they were wood. On the vases at each corner of the pediment, perches a large granite bird. *Murça*

Beyond Murça the road climbs up to the foothills of a rolling *serra* with barley growing in the great pastures. At Mirandela a medieval bridge spans the river Tua. An attractive town, with lovely houses and the splendid 17th century Tavora palace, now the town hall. The triple façade is highest in the centre and, though the great pediments are decorated with flambeaux and coats of arms, the whole building gives an oddly Dutch impression. *Mirandela*

Between Mirandela and Braganza, the road continues over the arable lands of the Serra da Nogueira. The road lies high, at about 1200 ft, but even so there are numbers of willows and poplars.

Braganza

Although so remote, the city of Braganza is a prosperous, cheerful town, self-sufficient and secure in its sense of historical import-ance. The old town crowns a hilltop and is still surrounded by medieval walls and towers. The great castle keep rises up above the 12th century town hall, one of the very rare Romanesque civic buildings still standing. The edifice is built over a water cistern and inside, a stone bench runs right round under the small, unglazed, arched windows. Yet another Iron Age boar stands in a small public garden in the old town, but it is smaller than that in Murça, and the shaft of the very tall medieval pillory has been driven through his body.

Abade de
Baçal
Museum

The Abade de Baçal, who was the parish priest of a small village near Braganza at the end of the last century and the beginning of this, made it his life's work to discover all he could about the city and its surroundings and published his researches in a work of 11 volumes. It was he who first drew attention to the existence of the *Marranos*, the Jews who at the time of the Inquisition which, incidentally, never took root in Portugal as it did in Spain, fled into the wild country around Braganza, their descendants still practis-ing a curious mixture of Jewish and Christian rites.

The museum, named after him and installed in the former episcop-al palace, possesses not only remarkable archaeological remains, including a collection of granite pigs from remote villages, but also paintings and sculpture, furniture, and 19th century bronzes. The coins are of particular interest to collectors, as they include a complete set of Portuguese coinage up to the proclamation of the Republic in 1910. In the old episcopal chapel, with a lovely painted ceiling, there are fine vestments and a good canvas in the classical retable.

The churches of Braganza are most interesting. The cathedral, formerly the Jesuit church, has a beautiful fan-traceried Gothic roof with unusual red bosses in the groining. The sacristy is particularly remarkable, with scenes from the life of St Ignatius in the coffered ceiling and above the vestment chests, in addition to two life-size polychrome figures of St Ignatius and St Francis. The Misericordia, near the cathedral, was founded in 1418, thus mak-ing it one of the earliest in the country. The buildings are no longer used for their original purpose, a new hospital having been built just outside the town. In the church is a splendid golden Renaiss-ance four-storeyed retable in high relief. São Vicente has a charm-ing, long side façade onto the street and an unusually late ceiling dated 1886, with vivid figures of the Evangelists, and Christ with two soldiers, again showing how artistic trends reached Portugal and were explored in country districts far later than in the rest of Europe. São Bento has a ceiling painted with classical and architectural features in a superbly wild way.

The city is so pretty, with low, whitewashed houses and elegant squares, that this also would be a pleasant place to stay, particular-ly in the late spring, when wild flowers cover the high ground with

vivid colour. The *Pousada de São Bartolomeu* is outside the town
(tel. (0092) 22493), but in the city itself there are the *Hotel Bragança*, the *Albergaria Santa Isabel* and a number of reasonably comfortable pensions.

*Accommoda-
tion*

The road, 60 miles in length, from Braganza to Chaves, winds
through marvellous country. Do not be put off by the long, somewhat dreary village of Vinhais, some 20 miles along this road, for at
the end of the village street, alongside flights of wide steps to the
south, is a long Baroque façade with two churches set in it. The
lower part is the Convent of São Francisco, onetime seminary of
the Diocese of Braganza. The church has a beautiful ceiling and
fine marbled boiseries. The relic chapels are most peculiar, the
sacristy is superb, the red and gold carved backs of the vestment
chests curve upwards and inwards to meet the line of the ceiling.
The upper church of the Third Order of St Francis, has one of the
finest painted ceilings in Portugal with architectural features of
urns and flowers, depicted in delicate colours on an off-white
ground. The altars are golden jewels and there is a wealth of
polychrome statues.

Vinhais

Chaves, only six miles south of Spain, with a frontier post at Vila
Verde da Raia was, as its name implies, the key to northern
Portugal and was originally fortified after it was captured from the
Moors in 1160, to ensure command of the valley of the Tamega
fronting the Spanish fortress of Verin. The Vaubon-style ramparts
were added in the 17th century. It is known that the Romans
appreciated the thermal springs in this city, and Trajan built a
bridge over the river. This bridge still survives and on the miles-
tones at the southern end, can be seen legible Roman inscriptions.

Chaves

The castle, with a tooth-battlemented keep was built by King Diniz
in the 14th century. Below the castle, the Praça de Camões is
surrounded by delightful houses, many with lovely ironwork balconies on the top floor. At right angles, the Misericordia church is
early Baroque, with huge panels of blue and white *azulejos* with
scenes from the New Testament reaching high up to the painted
ceiling. Some early canvases in the sacristy are worth seeing.

Castle

The *Estalagem de Santiago* is four star and there are other hotels
and pensions.

A mile or two outside Chaves, on the road to Outeiro Seco, stands
the perfect Romanesque church of Nossa Senhora de Azinheira. In
the interior are some of the best 16th century frescoes in Portugal.

On the road to Valpaços, balanced in such a way that a child can
make it rock, is a huge granite boulder, the *pedra bulideira.*

*Pedra
Bulideira*

West of Chaves, the road which ultimately reaches Braga, passes
high above the great man-made lake of the Barragem do Alto
Rabagão. Before this long stretch of water is reached, a turning

north goes to the beautiful and castellated hill town of Montalegre. It is dominated by the high keep of the late-medieval castle. The narrow streets are filled with friendly people, delighted to see a foreign face. The two churches have agreeable rustic features but the charm of the place lies in its extreme remoteness.

South-east of Braganza there are some interesting towns on the way to Miranda do Douro. The road goes through undulating country with vast views, until the ruins of the castle of Outeiro crowning a low hill come into sight. The small town is dominated by a large church, that of Santo Cristo. The façade is a strange mixture with a Manueline doorway, surmounted by a Gothic rose window within a pair of much later towers. The interior is fine with a groined roof, a Baroque high altar and lovely sacristy, the coffered ceiling containing charming primitive canvases of the life of Christ.

This part of Portugal is rich in minerals, mainly copper and wolfram and there are still remains of Roman workings for copper.

The next place of any size, Vimioso, was for long a key town in the defence of the country and suffered many engagements with the Spaniards. The town is appealing with fine houses emblazoned with the coats of arms of their builders.

South of Vimioso a road leads through Campo de Viboras until it ends at the ruined castle of Algoso, built on a high bluff, from which there is a fantastic view. An early *pelourinho* stands in the main square. The road from Vimioso to Miranda do Douro goes through high fertile land with some vineyards. All this part of the country is excessively cold in winter and hot in summer.

A few miles before Miranda, the village of Malhadas is known as a centre for the breeding of the rare Miranda cattle, marvellously adapted to this high country of climatic extremes. There is a medieval cross in the village square and the parish church contains traces of early frescoes.

Miranda do Douro

Soon, in the distance, the grey mass of Miranda do Douro can be seen ahead, situated on a hill above the river Douro, which has been dammed below the town for one of the many hydro-electric projects which supply the country with electricity. Between the still largely-walled city and the long artificial lake is the *Pousada de Santa Caterina*, (tel. (091) 55) an ideal place to stay for motorists who want to explore this countryside.

The city, with under two thousand inhabitants, is very unusual. Entered by medieval gateways, the narrow streets are lined with splendid 14th and 15th century houses, the most notable being in the Rua da Costanilha. The castle with the exception of the keep, is largely in ruins, but even so it towers over the town; at one time it was Wellington's headquarters in the Peninsular War. The Renaissance cathedral is well worth visiting and has a lovely organ, a fine Spanish high altar retable enclosing dozens of polychrome carved wood figures, painted landscapes behind the choir stalls and, in the south transept, the statue of the Menino Jesus da Cartolinha, or the Child Jesus in a Silk Hat, dressed in a suit with a top hat and a large bow tie. This touching and amusing image is much loved by the local people who, over the years, have presented it with a large wardrobe. By the cathedral are the ruins of the episcopal palace, which was destroyed by a fire in 1706 and from the terrace outside the cathedral there is a marvellous view of the gorge across which the great dam was built.

Living in the most remote city in Portugal, the people of Miranda have developed their own dialect called *Mirandes*, and their own dances. The *Pauliteiros* is danced by men in white kilts, black shirts and flower-bedecked black hats. It is a Stick Dance, the men striking the sticks they hold in each hand, to mark the rhythm of the complicated steps. The *Romaria* on September 7th and 8th to the chapel of Nossa Senhora do Nazo, north of the city, is the best place in which to see this and other characteristic local dances such as the *Pingacho*, a kind of ballet, the *Galandum* for both men and women, round dances like the *Geriboila* and pastoral dances for couples. Even now many of the older men and women of this region wear heavy black wool cloaks, woven in the cottages, as is the linen from which the men's shirts and women's blouses are made. Both the cloaks and the linen are highly embroidered. *Stick Dance*

The river Douro forms the frontier with Spain from a few miles above Miranda down to the Beira Alta where it turns sharply inland at Barca d'Alva. There is a series of hydro-electric dams along its whole length, the largest being that at Miranda.

South of Miranda and south of the village of Duas Igrejas are curious paleolithic remains with carvings on the exterior and interior walls of a rocky cave. *Duas Igrejas*

Off the main road from Miranda down to Mogadouro, a very secondary road to the north leads to Penas Roias, a tiny village clustered around a ruined Templar's castle with a high keep towering over the landscape. *Penas Roias*

Once the flourishing centre of the silkworm trade, Mogadouro is now a pleasant cheerful looking town with another ruined Templar's castle, some agreeable churches and the buildings of a former Franciscan Monastery, which were rebuilt after a fire in the last century. *Mogadouro*

Due west of Mogadouro, along a beautiful but very twisting road, the town of Vila Flor is dominated by the parish church containing Baroque features and a good sacristy. In the town, by the Miseri- *Vila Flor* cordia chapel, is the lovely Solar dos Lemos, a perfect 18th century house with florid granite windows set in startling whitewash. A public library and museum was founded by a local couple and contains documents and books relating to the town as well as paintings, furniture, coins and church plate.

Torre de Moncorvo

Although close to one of the largest deposits of iron ore in Europe in the Serra do Reboredo, Moncorvo due south of Vila Flor is a sleepy town with a 17th century parish church and a Misericordia, the former with a solid square tower in the centre of the façade. The building is large and high with three aisles and bears comparison with the cathedral in Miranda do Douro. There is a sculptured retable to a side altar and a 17th century polychrome wood triptych of the life of the Virgin and St Anne. There are numbers of fine houses in the narrow streets of the old town.

Freixo de Espada à Cinta

Back to the frontier and south of Mogadouro is the strangely named Freixo de Espada à Cinta. Set in a fertile plain surrounded by mountain ranges, the town is dominated by a high hexagonal tower at the side of the parish church – all that remains of the once important medieval fortifications. The interior of the 16th century church recalls the great groined roof of Jeronimos near Lisbon, though the columns dividing the three aisles are not highly decorated. There is a series of 16 exceptionally fine paintings attributed to Grão Vasco in beautiful Baroque frames. The Annunciation is particularly lovely, the Virgin kneeling at a low Gothic cupboard by a curtained bed, with a landscape seen through a glassless window. The Misericordia contains attractive gaudy retables and in the former hospital there is a pleasant home for the elderly.

So, Tras-os-Montes, the most remote and unknown part of Portugal brings to an end this Travellers Guide to a country which the enquiring and enterprising visitor will find as rewarding and full of interest as many more famous places.

Index

142

143

144